MW01247890

Happy Cooking! Best Loved Italian!

Rosalie

To Pam!

Rosalie Fiorino Harpole

ROSALIE
SERVING
BEST LOVED
ITALIAN

Italian Cream Cake
on page 206

Italian Stuffed Sausage Bread
on page 115

ROSALIE FIORINO HARPOLE

ROSALIE
SERVING
BEST LOVED
ITALIAN

Graphic Design by:

    Dennis Fiorini

    Grafx Gourmet

    grafxgourmet@yahoo.com

Photography by:

    St. Louis Color

Proofread by:

    William R. Harpole and Kathleen Fiorini

Published by:

    Rosalie Fiorino Harpole

    58 Madden Rd., Troy, MO 63379

Manufactured in the United States of America

ISBN: 9780757746703

Library of Congress Cataloging in Publication Data

Copyright ©2015 by Rosalie Fiorino Harpole

All rights reserved

Contents

White Pizza with Garlic Chicken
& Spinach on page 120

DEDICATION

- This is my third cookbook and again I give honor to the Lord, Jesus Christ for the health, strength and fortitude He gives me daily. When I give Him my best, He gives me His supreme!

- To my beloved husband Bill who again endured months of typing, changing, editing and compiling this project. He still takes me on dates, buys me flowers and packs my suitcase.

- To my three children and their spouses: Scott and Jennifer, Jeff and Tami, and Dana and David. What fantastic kids! Who in their own right are ministers, musicians, singers and writers.

- And to the eleven grandchildren and one great grandchild, who keep me every day entertained, enlightened, and entangled in their lives. They are from oldest to the youngest: Taylor Ryan Harpole, Ross David Harpole, Roman Anthony Harpole, Grant Nehemiah Carleton Harpole, Max Geoffrey Harpole, Reagan Brack Harpole, Alexandra Von Harpole, Elijah Harpole Schultz, Nicholas Fiorino Harpole, Sebastian Durniat Schultz, Naomi Fiorino Schultz, and our great grandchild, Gia Ryan Harpole.

Acknowledgements

Someone once said, "Don't aim for success if you want it, just do what you love and believe in, and it will come naturally." I have been so blessed to be raised in an Italian family, with a mother who loved to cook and entertain her guests. She never tired of making her Sunday dinner special: mostaccioli covered in her wonderful red sauce, featuring the best juicy meatballs one could ever hope to experience. She would load the sauce with other meat too, like—believe it or not—pork rib tips and even chicken. The bread was started early, about 5:00 AM, and the smell of her kitchen alone would bring people swarming to our house. Every Sunday I would be amazed at the different people, along with family, that would find their way to our home.

She was successful in what she did because she loved doing it, and her greatest joy was serving her wonderful food to anyone willing to sit down at her table. When I think of who to acknowledge for my love of cooking, it has to be my mother, Ann Fiorino. She is no longer with me, but watching her in her kitchen day after day made me who I am today. I have written many articles about her and her cooking, one of which you will find in the Cakes, Cookies & Creams section of this cookbook entitled *My Mother's Christmas Cookies*.

I acknowledge all the great people that have crossed my path and given me opportunities to share my talents. I thank the Dierbergs's School of Cooking, located in St. Louis, Missouri, and in Illinois for allowing me to teach cooking classes and advertise my cookbooks. Also, I'm thankful for Barnes & Nobel who have always welcomed me for their annual book signings. I have had the opportunity to advertise my *Rosalie Serving Italian*, and *Rosalie Serving Country* cookbooks on "The Hill" located in the South St. Louis area. This is the well-known Italian district, lined with famous Italian markets, many of which have allowed my cookbooks to be a part of their agenda.

I thank the many churches, schools, libraries, and organizations that have allowed me to come speak on topics of preserving family values, using food as a great part of the relationships in our lives. Without these open doors, I would never have had the opportunity to share my story of growing up with immigrant parents from Italy and how I came to love to cook, and eventually write three cookbooks.

Again, I give credit to my husband Bill who does the taste-testing for all the food dishes, gives me his honest opinion, and then brags to everyone who will stop and listen about how great his wife cooks. Sometimes he totally embarrasses me! He also does a great job editing.

Thanks to my graphic designer Dennis Fiorini who never ceases to amaze me with his talent of laying out beautiful cookbooks. Your work is much appreciated.

Thanks to my food photographer Guillermo Gomez, owner of St. Louis Color Photography, and his accomplished assistant Sonia Dea. I thank you for the many photo shoots of my food, family, and table settings. The first thing most everyone says when they pick up my cookbooks is, "who did these beautiful food photos?" Thank you, Guillermo, what would a cookbook be without pictures?

Thanks to all my coworkers at the Lincoln County Medical Center in Troy, Missouri where I work part-time as a registered nurse, for taste-testing many of the dishes in this cookbook. You guys seemed to look forward to a new "dish" to taste.

Thanks to the printer. You did a fantastic job!

I must say a final thanks to the many chefs and cooks who have inspired me. Some from my own family, and others who are well known, like Lidia Matticchio Bastianich, who is a renowned Italian cook and is acclaimed for her research, customs, and history of Italian cuisine. She wrote, among many cookbooks, *Lidia's Italian Table*. I also enjoy Giada De Laurentiis and Mark Bittman, both very accomplished in cooking and writing cookbooks.

Rosalie's Italian Salad with
Balsamic Vinaigrette on page 68

ENDORSEMENTS

Viviano & Sons located "On the Hill" in St. Louis, Missouri is the oldest Italian Food Market, and is always delighted when Rosalie sets up her table in our store. She not only has a successful book signing, but brings us a treat from her new Italian cookbook. We loved the *Cannoli Cake* and are still raving about the *Mascarpone Frosting*. Good luck and best wishes on your new *Rosalie Serving Best Loved Italian* cookbook.

John Viviano, CEO

Thank you so much for your newsletter about the *Good Old Days*. I always look forward to your monthly email letter and recipe to share with our family. This month brought back many wonderful memories for me. I've already forwarded it to our daughter, who has eight children. She and I, as well as our teenage granddaughter, all have your cookbooks and look forward to more in the future. Keep those cheerful, amusing letters coming and all of your delicious recipes!

Mary Delhaute, Beecher City, IL

Rosalie's cookbooks are about simplicity, comfort and good times with family and friends, which is why her cookbook classes have been so incredibly popular since 2008. Her food tastes like home cooking and because of it, our customers enjoy her recipes as well as her wonderful family photos and hearty-warming stories. These are the recipes she cooks at home—full of wonderful flavors and love. What could be better? You're sure to treasure each recipe and story.

Patty Tomaselli, Administrative Assistant, Dierberg's School of Cooking

As a Barnes & Nobel Community Relations Manager, I handle the author events in my store. One of my favorites has always been Rosalie Harpole. Her personality and ability to engage with my customers makes her the dream guest. But, my selfishly personal reason is that I LOVE to cook, and Rosalie's cookbooks are eminently usable, practical, and geared to the home cook. I'm always happy to welcome a new Rosalie Harpole cookbook to my store.

Deborah Horn, Community Relations Manager, Fenton, Missouri Barnes & Noble

Rosalie's cooking has been legendary in our community for years. We were thrilled when she put her tried and true recipes to print for all to enjoy. We can guarantee this newest effort, *Rosalie Serving Best Loved Italian* cookbook, will not disappoint! P.S. Her *Italian Fried Cabbage* is heavenly!

Rebecca Sheller, Halo and Wings Christian Book & Gift Store, Troy, MO

We at DiGregorio's are a family-owned Italian Food Market located on "The Hill" in St. Louis, Missouri. We have "a little taste of Italy" in every corner of our store, so when Rosalie comes for book signings, she adds to the Italian atmosphere. Her first cookbook, *Rosalie Serving Italian*, was first introduced at DiGregorio's and has been a great success on our book shelves. Our customers love that she gives out samples of her wonderful Italian cakes, and her bubbly personality grabs their hearts. Thank you also for the wonderful *Italian Cream Cake* . . . our staff devoured it. We are looking forward to her new cookbook, *Rosalie Serving Best Loved Italian*.

Toni Ribaudo, DiGregorio's Owner

It has been such a pleasure to get to know Rosalie Harpole over the years. She has been a loyal customer for many years, and we have gratefully been able to supply many of the items from which she prepares such wonderful fare. We have enjoyed all of Rosalie's cookbooks and sincerely look forward to this, her newest one. We often have a preview of the books in the form of sampling the recipes for many of the photo shoots. Such great information and recipes from a sweet, sweet lady!

Ellyn Theobald, Sugar Grove Growers Inc. Troy, MO

I have had the pleasure of working with Rosalie for several years, and I must say she is a delight to patients and coworkers. I jokingly one day asked her to make me a pineapple upside-down cake, and was so surprised when it showed up one day on my desk. I have to say it was absolutely delicious! She demonstrates the same caring professionalism in her cooking as well in her nursing care. God bless.

Dr. Stephen Lillard, Lincoln County Medical Center, Troy, MO

Rosalie and her cooking have been legendary at our hospital and in our community for years. Now, after two wonderful cookbooks, TV cooking appearances and St. Louis area-wide cooking classes, Rosalie is well-known for her delicious recipes. I gave copies of Rosalie's first cookbook *Rosalie Serving Italian* to my wife and three daughters. Soon after trying those recipes, all our friends were requesting a copy of their own. The second cookbook *Rosalie Serving Country* was just as phenomenal. We are all eagerly awaiting Rosalie's third book *Rosalie Serving Best Loved Italian*. You can be sure there will be many more great treats to come.

Dale L. Reinker, D.O., FACOFP, Former Chief Medical Officer, Lincoln County Medical Center Troy, MO

We, here at Festa Italiano, also known as Viviano's Italian Market and Restaurant in Fenton, Missouri, always welcome Rosalie and her cookbooks. She is the "Festa Italiano" with her electric personality and ability to connect with every customer. We love the book signings and especially the samples of her Italian cakes. Thank you, Rosalie, for the beautiful cookbooks, and we look forward to your newest adventure, *Rosalie Serving Best Loved Italian*.

Michael Viviano, owner, and CEO of Festa Italiano, Fenton, MO

INTRODUCTION

When my first cookbook, *Rosalie Serving Italian*, went out of print for the third time, rather than reprinting, I decided to write a brand new cookbook. At first it would be a holiday cookbook, featuring my favorite recipes for all the well-known American holidays. The title would be *Rosalie Serving Holidays*. This project went on for about two years, with photo shoots capturing everything from *Irish Soda Bread* to *Mexican Fried Rice*. The pictures were beautiful, and the food was delicious, but everywhere I went, especially during book signings, people would ask where they could get a copy of *Rosalie Serving Italian*.

There was just no way around it . . . another Italian cookbook had to be in my future. Still undecided, during one of the photo shoots for the holiday cookbook, my photographer Guillermo Gomez suggested a brand new Italian cookbook, keeping the old classics but adding many new popular American/Italian favorites. After much prayer and consideration, I felt very impressed to take his advice, and all the new recipes began to take life. We began shooting pictures of *Chicken Gnocchi Soup*, *White Pizza with Garlic Chicken and Spinach*, *Baked Rigatoni with Sausage and Red/Cream Sauce*, and many exciting new desserts, such as *Rosalie's Cannoli Cake* and the *Black Beauty Chocolate Cake with Hazelnut Filling* and *Rich Chocolate Frosting*. The day after each photo shoot, I would deliver lunches to the community workers with the food previously photographed.

Every time I would go into town, people would stop and ask, "When is that new cookbook coming out?"

Month after month, I would be researching and collecting recipes, typing and compiling, pulling out, and adding in some of the most popular of the Italian cuisine. My hope would be that I could strike a chord in someone's childhood memory by including a dish they grew up loving. Most Italians, depending on their roots and the part of Italy their ancestors came from, have their own special way to make even basic red sauce. I must say my cooking tends to be more of the Sicilian cuisine, but hopefully, you may find among these recipes something from your heritage. For instance, take the *Creamy Mushroom Risotto*. Even though I was not raised with risotto, I tried to find a recipe that most everyone would love, and after making this dish over and over to make it my own, I loved it so much that it made me sad my mother never caught on to it.

I have enjoyed writing this cookbook, and as with the other two, there will be lots of pictures showing off my beloved family. Another passion of mine is writing, and I do hope you enjoy many of the articles taken from past newsletters and blogs. Remember, food is the bridge to relationships and my desire is that your family grows closer making and enjoying these recipes.

God bless, and happy cooking Italian.

Rosalie Serving Best Loved Italian

Happy Cooking Italian

From Rosalie's Kitchen to Yours

When making your favorite Italian dish, one thing is for sure . . . you have to be ready! This means that your cupboard must be stocked with all the Italian staples that constitute a perfect dish. Oils, cheeses, fresh garlic, and dried herbs are a must. The following suggestions may be helpful, and at least you will know some of the favorite things I love to have on hand.

- **Olive Oil:** Imported olive oils are wonderful, but can be expensive. My favorite is *Bertolli Classico*, and it comes both in extra virgin and 100% pure mild. Use the extra virgin for sauces, salads, and vegetable and meat dishes. Use the 100% pure to bake with. I use the milder olive oil in all of my cake recipes.

- **Vinegars:** Red wine, balsamic, and apple cider are my favorite vinegars. These vinegars mixed with extra virgin olive oil are the basics for a great salad dressing.

- **Chicken and Beef Stocks:** These stocks lend great flavor to soups, sauces, and gravies. My favorite is *Kitchen Basics*. It is full-bodied and great tasting.

- **Pastas:** Homemade fresh pasta is an experience everyone should have, and in the pasta section, you will find my family recipe. My favorite brand for dry pastas is *Barilla*. For a creative dish of pasta any time, have on hand a variety of types. Some of my favorites are: penne, angel hair, linguine, fettuccine, rigatoni, bow-ties, vermicelli, and spaghetti, both thick and thin. Acini de pepe, ditalini, and small shells make great add-ins for soups.

- **Cheeses:** There is just nothing better to garnish Italian dishes than fresh grated cheese. My favorites are: Pecorino Romano, Mozzarella, Parmesan, Asiago, and Fontina. Many of these come in block form and are perfect for fresh grating. Buffalo Mozzarella is packed in milk and is a must for focaccia bread and pizzas. It is also delicious in *Caprese Salad*.

- **Garlic:** Nothing can replace the taste of fresh garlic. Look for bulbs with a little purple tinge for the freshest cloves. I do not recommend bottled brine garlic; it can never take the place of the "bite" you get with fresh garlic.

- **Fresh Herbs:** There is no comparison to fresh herbs. Grow them in the summer, and freeze them for use during the winter months. My favorite to grow are: parsley (curly and flat leaf), basil, peppermint, rosemary, chives, and oregano. If using dried herbs, replace them in your pantry every six months for the best flavor. Always have fennel seed on hand. This herb is a must for the best meatballs ever!

- **Red Pepper Flakes:** This is one seasoning you will use often. It is great in pasta sauces, on pizzas and on roasted vegetables. Be sure it is on your shelf.

- **Coarse Garlic Salt with Parsley:** This staple is my favorite seasoning. I use Lawry's coarse garlic salt with parsley. This is great on all meats and fish. It is also good on vegetables, whether grilled or roasted.

- **Sea Salt & Coarse Black Pepper:** Kosher salt and pepper grinders are easy and wonderful to use. Be sure to have them on the table for the guests to use on their pasta and salad dishes.

- **Bread Crumbs:** Bread crumbs are a must to have on hand. They are used in so many dishes; as fillers, and for coating meats and vegetables. Stock both plain and Italian.

APPETIZERS
&BEVERAGES

I call the appetizers "fun food" because it's the part of the meal when everyone is hungry and anticipating what the passing trays will hold. Italians love to serve appetizers, and may even call them "antipasta." They could be anything from a block of cheese and a knife, where you just cut off a sliver of cheese and eat it with a piece of bread and fresh purple grapes, or more formal, like the Italian Stuffed Sausage Mushrooms, where hot bubbling mushrooms are stuffed with sweet Italian sausage and spices.

Growing up, I still have visions of my mother taking a hot loaf of bread out of the oven and holding it by a towel, so she wouldn't burn her hand slicing it. She would pour olive oil over the sliced bread and sprinkle it with cheese. Then, if she had extra meatballs cooked up in sauce, everyone could get a hot meatball right out of the sauce and put it on a slice of hot bread. She would only do this to appease us while she was still working on the main meal. This was her "appetizer." It was such a great memory for me, that I included my Italian Turkey Meatballs in Marinara Sauce served on Italian bread.

The only problem with appetizers is that it is very hard to stop with just one. Consider the Best Spinach and Artichoke Dip with Toasted Pita Wedges. When I served this during a cooking class, I had to warn everyone that there would only be one serving; otherwise, I knew they wouldn't be able to stop. It was so good!

Spoil your guests, and serve up these wonderful appetizers. And don't forget the great beverages like Creamy Hot Chocolate with Whipped Cream Garnish, and of course the wonderful Cranberry Orange Fizz.

Time: 30 minutes

ITALIAN STUFFED
SAUSAGE MUSHROOMS

Note: *These wonderful stuffed mushrooms are a mouthful of Italian flavor. They are perfect for any party or gathering or for no reason at all. Your family will love you for making these . . . yum!*

1 pound large white button mushrooms, about 30

1 pound ground Italian sausage

Olive oil

¼ cup plain bread crumbs

⅓ cup grated Parmesan cheese

2 cloves garlic, chopped

¼ teaspoon crushed red pepper flakes

¼ teaspoon coarse sea salt

¼ teaspoon coarse ground black pepper

2 tablespoons curly parsley, chopped

⅓ cup red bell pepper, diced

2 to 3 tablespoons olive oil

⅓ cup marinated artichokes hearts, chopped

1 cup shredded provolone or mozzarella cheese, divided

Olive oil

1. Preheat oven to 400 degrees. Rinse mushrooms in cool water; pat dry. Remove stems and gently clean out cavity, being careful to keep cap intact; set shells aside. Fry sausage in skillet in olive oil for 5 to 6 minutes, or until meat is no longer pink; do not overcook sausage.

2. In medium bowl, place the sausage, bread crumbs, cheese, garlic, crushed red pepper flakes, salt, and pepper; mix well. Next, add the parsley, red bell pepper, olive oil, artichoke hearts, and ⅓ cup of the provolone or mozzarella cheese. Stir the stuffing with a fork, or mix with clean hands. If the stuffing is too stiff or does not come together, add a little more olive oil, or juice from the artichokes.

3. Stuff each cap with stuffing to a little overflowing. Place mushrooms on a dry 18-inch by 12-inch cookie sheet and drizzle a little olive oil over each mushroom. Place pan in hot oven for 15 minutes. Remove from oven and use the remaining ⅔ cup shredded mozzarella cheese to top each mushroom. Place back in oven and bake another 30 seconds to slightly melt cheese. Remove, and let cool for 5 minutes; serve warm. Makes 30 mushrooms.

Time: 15 minutes

BEST SPINACH & ARTICHOKE DIP WITH TOASTED PITA WEDGES

Note: *This is an old faithful that has never lost its popularity. It is still as wonderful as ever, with a satin feel in your mouth and bits of warm spinach and artichoke combined in luscious cheeses. Serve with your favorite toasted breads or crackers.*

¼ cup butter

½ onion, finely chopped

3 cloves garlic, finely chopped

1 (10-ounce) package of fresh baby spinach

1 (14-ounce) can marinated artichoke hearts, drained and chopped

¾ to 1 cup whole milk

1 (8-ounce) package cream cheese

1 (4-ounce) package Feta cheese, crumbled and divided

1 cup shredded Parmesan cheese

1 (10-ounce) bag shredded Monterey Jack cheese, divided

¼ teaspoon red pepper flakes

Pita wedges, toasted

1. Preheat oven to 400 degrees. Place the butter in large skillet and sauté the onion and garlic for 5 to 6 minutes, until golden in color.

2. Add the spinach, and stir until slightly wilted. Add the artichoke hearts and work into the spinach mixture. Keep heat on low simmer and add the milk. While milk is heating, add the cream cheese, and 2 ounces of the Feta cheese. Stir until melted into the milk mixture, about 2 to 3 minutes. Add the Parmesan cheese and 8 ounces of the Monterey Jack cheese. Continue to stir until the cheeses are melted in, and the mixture becomes slightly bubbly, 2 to 3 minutes. Add the red pepper flakes; stir until smooth.

3. Remove from heat and place the dip in an oven-proof 9x13-inch serving dish and sprinkle the remaining Feta and shredded Monterey Jack over the top. Place in oven for 6 to 8 minutes, or until cheeses become golden and melted on top. Remove from oven and serve with toasted pita wedges. Makes 4 cups.

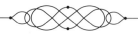

Time: 10 Minutes

STUFFED CHERRY PEPPERS

Note: *These little red and green stuffed peppers are very tasty, and will disappear quickly from your appetizer tray.*

1 (16-ounce) jar Mezzetta pickled sweet cherry peppers

2 slices provolone cheese, finely chopped

2 slices prosciutto, thinly sliced, or 2 slices Genoa salami, finely chopped

Drain peppers and with sharp knife, cut carefully around stem and remove. With a tiny spoon, scoop out the seeds. Mix the provolone and prosciutto together. Fill each cavity of the peppers to slightly overflowing. Place on tray and serve. Makes 12.

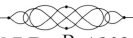
Time: 30 Minutes

FRIED RAVIOLI
WITH MARINARA SAUCE

Note: *Fried ravioli, also referred to as "toasted" ravioli, was originated in St. Louis, MO. It happened at a restaurant called Oldani's on "The Hill." As the story goes, the delicacy was stumbled upon when a ravioli was accidentally dropped into the fryer by Chef Fritz. Mickey Garagiola, older brother of Major League Baseball Hall-of-Famer Joe Garagiola, was actually at the bar during the mishap and was the first to taste the treat. Shortly after, the item began appearing on menus across "The Hill" neighborhood of St. Louis.*

1 recipe **Rosalie's Marinara Sauce** on page 160

½ pound frozen beef or cheese ravioli

1 tablespoon salt

3 eggs, beaten

⅔ cup plain bread crumbs

⅔ cup grated Parmesan cheese

2 cloves garlic, chopped fine

¼ cup fresh curly parsley, chopped

½ teaspoon salt

¼ teaspoon ground black pepper

½ cup olive oil

Parmesan cheese

1. Prepare the marinara sauce as directed; set aside. Boil ravioli in a 4-quart pot of boiling water with salt added until tender, about 3 to 5 minutes. Drain gently; set aside. Place the beaten eggs in a large bowl and add the drained ravioli; stir gently.

2. Combine the bread crumbs, cheese, garlic, parsley, salt, and pepper, and place in a shallow pie plate. With a slotted spoon, lift the ravioli, about 3 to 4 at a time out of the egg mixture, and place in the bread crumbs; turn gently to coat on both sides. Continue until all are breaded and place on cookie sheet.

3. In large skillet, heat olive oil until medium-hot. Add several coated ravioli to the oil and fry until golden brown on both sides, 2 to 3 minutes. Remove to paper towel to drain. Transfer to large platter and sprinkle with grated Parmesan cheese. Serve plain or dipped in marinara sauce. Serves 4.

Time: 15 Minutes

ITALIAN TURKEY MEATBALLS
IN MARINARA SAUCE

Note: *These juicy meatballs are every bit as good made with ground turkey as they are with ground chuck. Topped with shredded mozzarella and placed on fresh Italian bread, they turn into awesome appetizers.*

1 recipe **Rosalie's Marinara Sauce**
  recipe found on page 160

1 pound white ground turkey

2 cloves garlic, chopped

¼ cup plain or Italian seasoned
  bread crumbs

¼ cup grated Parmesan cheese

2 tablespoons curly parsley, chopped

2 eggs

½ teaspoon fennel seeds

½ teaspoon salt

¼ teaspoon ground black pepper

Olive oil

Fresh Italian bread, sliced

Mozzarella shredded cheese

1. Prepare the marinara sauce as directed; set aside. Place turkey meat in medium bowl.

2. Add the garlic, bread crumbs, cheese, parsley, eggs, fennel seeds, salt, and pepper. Mix the turkey and above ingredients together, and make into 2-inch balls. Fry the balls in olive oil over medium heat to partially done, about 2 to 3 minutes on each side. Complete cooking meatballs in the marinara sauce until done, about another 6 to 8 minutes. Place one meatball on a small slice of Italian bread. Top with about 1 tablespoon mozzarella cheese. Add more sauce as desired. Makes 12.

Time: 10 Minutes

MARINATED OLIVE SALAD

Note: *Marinated olive salads can be very expensive to buy, but when made homemade, they are not only inexpensive, but very delicious. This is a wonderful antipasta.*

½ pound large green pitted Spanish olives

1 (12-ounce) jar pitted Kalamata olives, drained

¾ cup celery hearts, ½-inch slices

½ cup Genoa salami, ½-inch cubed

½ cup Fontina cheese, small cubed

½ cup pepperoncini peppers, stems removed

1 teaspoon garlic, chopped fine

½ teaspoon dried oregano

1 teaspoon coarse sea salt

¼ teaspoon cracked black pepper

¼ teaspoon crushed red pepper flakes

¼ cup extra virgin olive oil

2 teaspoons red wine or cider vinegar

Mix all ingredients together and place in a large jar or covered container. Shake container to coat the olives with the seasonings. Keep refrigerated for one or two days, then remove to large bowl and let come to room temperature. Serve with warm Italian bread. Makes about 4 cups salad.

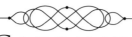

Time: 1 Hour

CAPONATA
(MARINATED EGGPLANT COMPOTE)

Note: *This is a classic Sicilian vegetable dish and can be used in many ways.*
Use it as an appetizer, or to accompany meat or fish entrées. If you love eggplant, you will love this.

1 large eggplant, unpeeled

3 teaspoons salt

1 medium onion, small quartered, about I cup

⅔ cup celery with leaves, cut into ½-inch slices

1 large red bell pepper, cored, seeded, and cut into 1-inch cubes

1 small zucchini, cubed, about 1 cup

1 large clove garlic, chopped

1 teaspoon coarse sea salt

¼ teaspoon ground black pepper

½ cup extra virgin olive, divided

1 (15-ounce) can diced tomatoes, with juice

¼ cup stuffed olives with pimento, halved

2 tablespoons golden raisins

¼ cup fresh basil leaves
   or ½ teaspoon dried basil

¼ cup cider vinegar

2 tablespoons sugar

1 tablespoon capers, drained and rinsed

1.   Cut end off eggplant, and slice into ½-inch circles. Soak eggplant in cool salted water with heavy bowl over top to keep eggplant submerged for about 20 minutes.

2.   Prepare the onion, celery, red bell pepper, zucchini, and garlic. Place in a large saucepan, and sprinkle with salt and pepper. Add ¼ cup olive oil and sauté together for 10 minutes. Vegetables will appear translucent.

3.   Rinse and drain the eggplant and cut into ½-inch cubes. In separate saucepan, add the remaining ¼ cup olive oil and sauté the eggplant for 10 minutes. Combine eggplant and the vegetables in the largest saucepan. Add the tomatoes, olives, raisins, and basil. Simmer together for 15 minutes.

4.   In small saucepan, place the vinegar, sugar, and capers. Cook together about 1 minute, or until mixture becomes syrupy. Add to the eggplant mixture and cook for another 5 minutes. Makes 4 cups.

Time: 10 Minutes

OLIVE OIL POPCORN

Note: *Once you make this popcorn, it will be hard to go back to microwave popcorn. Make a couple of batches, and keep in sealed gallon bags, ready for when you take the kids to the zoo. Delicious!*

1 (3-quart) heavy pot with lid

3 tablespoons olive oil

½ cup Orville Redenbacher's popping corn

Salt

Pour the olive oil and popcorn into the pot. Cover with lid and over medium heat, pop the corn, shaking the pot from side to side occasionally. When kernels stop popping, remove lid carefully. Transfer to large bowl. Add desired amount of salt and serve. Makes 10 cups.

Naomi Schultz

Time: 10 Minutes

CREAMY HOT CHOCOLATE WITH WHIPPED CREAM GARNISH

Note: *This hot chocolate is creamy and rich and goes well with your morning biscotti, or just any time you want a good hot drink.*

⅓ cup unsweetened cocoa powder

¾ cup sugar

Dash of salt

⅓ cup boiling water

3½ cups whole milk

1 teaspoon vanilla extract

1 cup heavy cream, divided

Pressurized whipped cream

Cinnamon sugar

Cinnamon sticks

1. In medium heavy saucepan, combine cocoa, sugar, salt. Add boiling water and bring to a gentle boil stirring constantly for 2 minutes.

2. Add the milk and vanilla. Continue to stir mixture until very hot, but not boiling. Pour hot chocolate into six cups; fill ⅔ full. Add ¼ cup cream to each mug and stir chocolate to a creamy texture. Garnish each mug with pressurized whipped cream, cinnamon sugar and cinnamon sticks. Makes 6 servings.

Time: 10 Minutes

CHOCOLATE ESPRESSO WITH WHIPPED CREAM AND CHOCOLATE SPRINKLES

Note: *If you love chocolate and coffee, you will love this perfect chocolate coffee.*

6 cups brewed espresso

6 teaspoons Hershey's cocoa, divided

6 teaspoons honey, divided

3 teaspoons pure vanilla, divided

6 tablespoons vanilla coffee creamer, divided

Pressurized whipping cream

Chocolate sprinkles, or curls

Brew coffee, and pour into 6 cups. Add 1 teaspoon of cocoa and 1 teaspoon of honey to each of the 6 cups; stir to dissolve. Add ½ teaspoon vanilla and 1 tablespoon vanilla coffee creamer; stir to combine. Top each cup with whipped cream and garnish with sprinkles or curls. Serve warm with your favorite pastry. Makes 6 cups.

Time: 10 Minutes

HOMEMADE CARAMEL LATTÉ

Note: *These homemade Lattés are easy to make and so delicious. Skip the coffee shop and save your money. You can enjoy them any time you wish. This recipe makes 1 cup at a time.*

2 tablespoons Hershey's Caramel Syrup

¾ cup hot espresso coffee

1 teaspoon turbinado sugar

½ cup half-and-half

Whipped cream

Caramel syrup

1 teaspoon turbinado sugar

1. Using a 10-ounce cup, pour in the caramel syrup; set aside. Make the espresso coffee with espresso machine, or use a very strong coffee. Pour the coffee into the cup with the caramel syrup and add the 1 teaspoon turbinado sugar. Stir well to dissolve syrup and sugar.

2. Steam the half-and-half in the microwave on high for 30 seconds; milk should be very hot but not scalded. Or, place the half-and-half into a small saucepan and heat to 120 degrees. Pour the half-and-half into the coffee and stir well. Spray whipped cream over the top of the coffee. Drizzle caramel syrup over the whipped cream. Sprinkle the turbinado sugar over the syrup. Serve while warm. Makes 1 (10-ounce) cup.

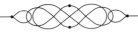
Time: 15 Minutes

CRANBERRY ORANGE FIZZ

Note: *I created this recipe while I was preparing Christmas dinner. I had some left-over cooked cranberries from making my Cranberry Trifle, and decided to pair it up with some orange soda. It was so good that I had to keep it in my recipe log. Everyone will love this!*

1 (12-ounce) package fresh cranberries

1 cup water

1 cup sugar

1 teaspoon cherry extract
    or 3 tablespoons maraschino cherry juice

2 (12-ounce) containers frozen pink lemonade

½ teaspoon red food coloring, optional

1 (1-liter) orange soda

Crushed ice

1. Cook the cranberries with the water and sugar over medium heat for about 8 to 10 minutes, or until the cranberries begin to pop and soften. Remove from heat and add the cherry extract if you have some, or add the maraschino cherry juice. Let the cranberries cool.

2. Divide the cranberries between two 10-cup pitchers, about 1 ½ cups to each. Make the lemonade by adding 3 cups water to each container; stir well to dissolve. Pour 3 cups lemonade into each of the pitchers with the cranberries. If desired, add the food coloring for a deeper red color. Divide the soda between the pitchers. Fill to the top with crushed ice. Makes two pitchers.

Time: 10 Minutes

RASPBERRY ZINGER TEA

Note: *This tea was served to me when I spoke for a large ladies group. It was so good and really beautiful in the goblet, and I just had to have the recipe from the Immanuel Lutheran Ladies Group in St. Charles, MO.*

1 (2-liter) bottle 7-up

5 Celestial Raspberry tea bags

Ice

Take 1 cup of soda out of the 2-liter bottle. Roll up each of the tea bags and insert into the bottle of 7-up. Place the cap back on the soda, and place in the refrigerator overnight, or for several hours. Remove cap and pour the tea over ice. Makes 8 cups.

Time: 10 Minutes

ITALIAN LEMON ICE

Note: *Lemon ice is an Italian tradition and a light touch after a large meal. For a large picnic crowd, use a 5-gallon container and increase the ingredients accordingly.*

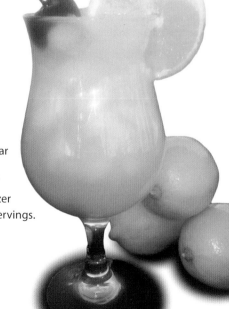

1 gallon crushed ice

1 large can frozen lemonade

Juice of 1 lemon

1 cup sugar, more or less for taste

Lemon slices

Maraschino cherries

Mix all ingredients together and serve in clear party cups or glasses. Garnish each glass with a lemon slice and a maraschino cherry. Cups of lemon ice can be made ahead and kept in freezer until ready to serve. Makes about 32 half-cup servings.

Puff Pastry with
Mascarpone Cherry Filling
on page 47

BREAKFAST & PASTRIES

Let's Make It Breakfast

Breakfast could be my favorite meal, and this no doubt stems from my childhood, and feasting on the homemade Italian sausage my father made in his butcher shop. We were always blessed to have plenty of meat, and mom made sure part of that meat was included in breakfast. She would make those awesome breakfast sandwiches, like, Italian Sausage & Egg Breakfast served on her Italian toasted sliced bread. These special breakfast meals were mainly reserved for the weekends, and especially on Sunday. Sometimes mom would make Frittata with Potatoes and Onions and this was a meal in itself. I can still taste the soft potatoes all wrapped up in the eggs and cheese . . . yum!

My father had a sweet tooth, and insisted mom make a pastry along with the breakfast meal. Since she loved to cook, she always obliged him, and of course all of us were the beneficiaries. She would make her Banana Bread with Vanilla Cream Icing and we would eat it still warm right out of the oven.

Later on in life, we moved our family right next door to hers when our children were young. Every Saturday, mom would make homemade pancakes, and call for our children to join her for breakfast. They delighted in her pancakes. While she didn't make them as elaborate as I would, they were heaven to my kids.

My wish is that you enjoy these breakfast items, and do try the Best Ever Scones with Almond Glaze. They are positively delicious!

MY FAVORITE TIPS FOR BREAKFAST:

1. **Eat breakfast!** Sounds simple, but many feel it is just too time-consuming. Actually, even a pastry and a cup of coffee is better than not eating at all. Breakfast is the most important meal, setting the stage for our metabolic system to get in gear for the day.

2. **Yogurt!** This is one of the best foods we can eat. Greek yogurt has been known to be a favorite in Puglia, Italy. It is a protein booster and a calcium builder. It also helps us to lose weight if we eat it daily. I just had to add my favorite Strawberry Greek Yogurt Parfait with Whipped Cream. I even included Homemade Crunchy Granola for the topping.

3. **Make your elaborate breakfast for the weekends** when your whole family can gather around the table. This is the time to bond with your family and make memories. My children have fond memories of my mother making them her Nutella Pancakes. I included this recipe in her memory.

4. **Italian Toast:** Did you know that day-old Italian bread is perfect for toast? It is like nothing else you have ever had. I describe it as crunchy and addictive. It works perfect on those days you are running late getting the kids to school. Pop slices in the toaster, butter it and sprinkle with cinnamon sugar . . . yum!

5. **Make it sweet!** Having a sweet cup of espresso with your breakfast satisfies your longings and completes the meal. Another way of celebrating your family!

Elijah Schultz and Freidman

Time: 20 Minutes

FRITTATA WITH SPINACH & PROSCIUTTO

Note: *This frittata is light and rich in spinach and prosciutto. Prosciutto is an Italian ham, and has a sweet, spicy flavor. If prosciutto is hard to find, regular ham can be used.*

1 tablespoon olive oil

1 tablespoon butter

2 tablespoons green onion, chopped fine

1 clove garlic, chopped fine

3 strips prosciutto, chopped

1 cup fresh spinach leaves, packed

½ teaspoon coarse sea salt

¼ teaspoon ground black pepper

6 large eggs

2 tablespoons half-and-half

1 tablespoon water

¼ cup Parmesan cheese

Parmesan cheese to garnish

Parsley sprigs

1. Preheat oven to 350 degrees. Put oil and butter in a 10-inch oven-proof skillet over medium heat until warm and blended. Sauté onion, garlic, and prosciutto together about 5 minutes, until onion is translucent and prosciutto is crisp. Add the spinach and cook together 1 to 2 minutes, until spinach is soft. Sprinkle with salt and pepper.

2. Beat the eggs with half-and-half and water until fluffy and fold in the cheese. Pour the eggs over the spinach mixture and cook on the stove undisturbed about 2 minutes, until eggs begin to set and bubble, but are still runny on top. Put skillet in oven for 8 minutes. Remove skillet and transfer frittata to a large round plate. The frittata should slide out of pan easily.

3. Garnish with additional cheese and parsley. Let the frittata set 2 minutes. Cut into pie slices. Serves 4 to 6.

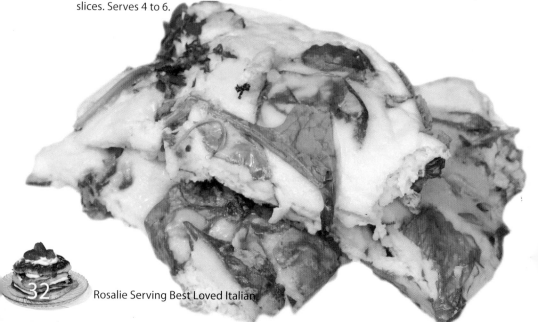

Time: 20 Minutes

FRITTATA WITH POTATOES & ONIONS

Note: *My mother would serve this frittata often as a main course.*
It was always warm and delicious with toasted bread and sliced tomatoes.

2 tablespoons olive oil

1 tablespoon butter

1 large potato, unpeeled and sliced thin
  or 4 small new potatoes, unpeeled and sliced thin

1 small onion, chopped small, about ½ cup

1 clove garlic, chopped fine

½ teaspoon salt

¼ teaspoon ground black pepper

6 eggs

2 tablespoons half-and-half

¼ cup Parmesan cheese

½ cup shredded mozzarella cheese

1 tablespoon fresh curly parsley, chopped

1 large tomato, optional

Parmesan cheese

Parsley sprigs

1. Preheat oven to 350 degrees. Put oil and butter in a 10-inch oven-proof skillet over medium heat until warm and blended. Sauté the potatoes, onion, and garlic in the olive oil and butter until the potatoes are tender, about 8 to 10 minutes. Sprinkle the potatoes with the salt and pepper while frying.

2. Beat the eggs with the half-and-half until fluffy and fold in the cheeses and parsley. Pour the egg mixture over the potatoes and cook undisturbed over medium heat about 2 minutes, until the eggs begin to set and bubble, but are still runny on top. Add the basil leaves on top. Place skillet in oven for 8 to 10 minutes. Remove skillet and transfer the frittata to a large round plate. The frittata should slide out of the pan easily.

3. Garnish with additional cheese and parsley. Serve with fresh vine-ripe tomato if desired. Let the frittata set about 2 minutes before slicing. Serves 6.

Time: 1½ Hours

ITALIAN STUFFED BREAKFAST BREAD

Note: *This amazing stuffed bread is an entire breakfast in itself. A big Italian loaf of bread, toasted on the outside and harboring the complete breakfast on the inside. This recipe comes from my arts and graphic designer, Dennis Fiorini.*

½ pound ground Italian sausage

1 to 2 tablespoons olive oil

½ cup button mushrooms, chopped thick slices

½ cup sweet multi-colored mini peppers, chopped small

½ medium onion, chopped small

¼ stick butter

6 large eggs, beaten fluffy

2 tablespoons water

1 (8-ounce) bag shredded mozzarella cheese

3 tablespoons Parmesan cheese

1 tablespoon Italian seasoning

1 (18x24-inch) sheet of aluminum foil

1 large loaf Italian or French bread

4 tablespoons Parmesan cheese, divided

Cookie sheet

1 cup shredded mozzarella, divided

1. Preheat oven to 350 degrees. Using large skillet, sauté the sausage in olive oil. Cook over medium heat until no longer pink, but not well done; crumble sausage as it cooks. Remove from pan, leaving drippings, and place into large bowl.

2. Add vegetables to pan drippings and sauté gently for about 3 minutes, careful not to over-cook vegetables, keeping them crisp tender. Remove vegetables to bowl with sausage.

3. Using a clean large skillet, add butter and allow to melt. Beat water in with eggs, keeping eggs light and fluffy; add eggs to butter. Allow eggs to "set" slightly, then using a spatula, lift and stir the eggs until slightly underdone, about 2 to 3 minutes. Eggs continue to cook after being removed. Place eggs in bowl with sausage and vegetables. Add the mozzarella, Parmesan, Italian seasoning, salt, and pepper to taste. Gently stir the mixture.

4. Place the aluminum foil on the counter. Cut loaf in half, hollowing out both sides to about ¼-inch from crust. Keep bread chunks for later use. Sprinkle 2 tablespoons Parmesan cheese into each loaf cavity. Divide the egg mixture between both halves. Roll both halves together with both hands and slightly crush together. Wrap in aluminum foil over and seal.

5. Place loaves on cookie sheet and bake for 30 minutes. Remove from oven and unwrap aluminum foil; sprinkle remaining two tablespoons Parmesan cheese and ½ cup mozzarella over loaf. Place uncovered back on aluminum foil in oven for 6 to 8 minutes, or until cheese melts and browns.

6. Remove from oven and place on cutting board to slice. Makes 8 to 10 servings.

Photo by Tim Burk

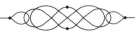
Time: 20 Minutes

ITALIAN SAUSAGE & EGG BREAKFAST

Note: *This Italian breakfast sandwich is so delicious, it may be addictive.*

1 recipe **Italian Homemade Salsiccia**
on page 174
or 1 pound ground sweet Italian
sausage

Olive oil

4 eggs

¼ cup olive oil

Stonemill steak seasoning

4 slices Italian bread

1 whole fresh vine-ripened tomato

1. Prepare Italian homemade sausage recipe as directed into patties, or use your favorite store-bought Italian ground sausage. Pour olive oil into large skillet to slightly cover bottom. Make the ground sausage into four large patties. Fry the patties in olive oil over medium heat until no longer pink, about 4 to 5 minutes on each side. Remove from pan and place on platter.

2. Using another clean skillet, fry eggs two at a time in the olive oil, reaching desired doneness. Remove cooked eggs to platter with sausage, and place one egg over each sausage patty. Sprinkle the egg with a little of the steak seasoning.

3. Toast the sliced Italian bread and place the egg and sausage patty over each slice of toasted bread. Place the sausage/egg sandwich on 4 individual plates. Garnish each sandwich with fresh sliced tomatoes. Makes 4 sausage/egg sandwiches.

Alexandra, Elijah,
and Reagan

Time: 20 Minutes

ITALIAN FRIED POTATOES & PEPPERS

Note: *These potatoes go well with breakfast, and are a complement to the Italian sausage and eggs.
If you do not like peppers, leave them out.*

2 large russet
  or Yukon gold potatoes, unpeeled

¼ cup green bell pepper, chopped small

¼ cup red bell pepper, chopped small

¼ cup chopped onion

3 tablespoons olive oil

1 teaspoon salt

½ teaspoon coarse black pepper

¼ teaspoon crushed red pepper flakes

Olive oil

Wash potatoes and pat dry. Cut potatoes into 1-inch wedges and place in large skillet, along with peppers and onions. Add the olive oil and over medium heat, stir-fry the potatoes, peppers and onions. Stir often until potatoes become golden brown, about 10 minutes. Add the salt, pepper, and crushed red pepper flakes while the potatoes are frying. When the potatoes are golden crusted, turn down heat and place lid over the potatoes to steam soft, about 5 minutes. Remove from heat and serve while warm. Serves 6.

Time: 20 Minutes

BUTTERMILK PANCAKES WITH STRAWBERRY CREAM FILLING

Note: *These pancakes will actually melt in your mouth, and the mascarpone is sweet and smooth sending this breakfast over the top*

1 cup strawberries, washed and sliced

¼ cup sugar

1 (8-ounce) carton mascarpone cheese

1 cup powdered sugar

1 cup heavy cream

1 teaspoon vanilla

1 ¼ all-purpose flour

1 teaspoon baking soda

1 teaspoon baking powder

½ teaspoon salt

1 tablespoon sugar

1 large egg

¼ cup melted butter

1½ cups buttermilk

½ cup white chocolate chips

Olive oil

Whipping cream, optional

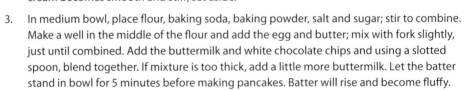

1. Place strawberries and sugar in a small bowl; toss together to coat strawberries. Cover bowl with clear wrap and place in refrigerator.

2. Make the cream filling by placing mascarpone cheese and powdered sugar in a mixing bowl; beat on low speed until combined and smooth. Add the whipping cream and vanilla. Beat on low to combine and then on high until the cream becomes smooth and stiff; set aside.

3. In medium bowl, place flour, baking soda, baking powder, salt and sugar; stir to combine. Make a well in the middle of the flour and add the egg and butter; mix with fork slightly, just until combined. Add the buttermilk and white chocolate chips and using a slotted spoon, blend together. If mixture is too thick, add a little more buttermilk. Let the batter stand in bowl for 5 minutes before making pancakes. Batter will rise and become fluffy.

4. Pour olive oil in the bottom of a large skillet. When oil is hot, pour about ⅓ cup batter in pan for each pancake. When bubbles appear on pancake, turn and fry on other side for 2 minutes. Pancakes should be golden brown and firm. Fry three pancakes and place on plate. Stuff the pancakes with the sweet cream filling, about 2 to 3 tablespoons. Top pancakes with sweetened strawberries. Garnish with whipped cream if desired. Makes 12 pancakes.

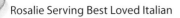

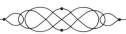
Time: 20 Minutes

CANDIED PECAN BUTTERMILK PANCAKES WITH NUTELLA

Note: *There is just nothing better than your own homemade buttermilk pancakes filled with candied pecans. Nutella is a favorite chocolate-hazelnut in the Italian cuisine.*

1⅔ cup buttermilk

1 teaspoon baking soda

3 egg yolks

¼ cup melted butter

1 teaspoon vanilla

1½ cups all-purpose flour

1 teaspoon baking powder

½ teaspoon salt

1 teaspoon sugar

3 egg whites

Olive oil

1 cup whole pecans, divided

2 tablespoons sugar

1 jar Nutella

1. Put buttermilk in a 2-cup bowl and add the baking soda, mixing with a fork to dissolve. Let stand for about 5 minutes. Beat egg yolks until fluffy and add the butter and vanilla. Add the buttermilk mixture to the egg mixture and whisk together.

2. Mix the flour, baking powder, salt, and sugar in a large bowl. Slowly add the wet ingredients to the dry ingredients, mixing together until both are incorporated and smooth.

3. Beat the egg whites until stiff and fold into the batter with a sweeping motion from bottom and over top. Let the batter stand 5 minutes.

4. Place pecans in dry skillet and heat to medium heat. Sprinkle the sugar over the pecans and stir constantly about 2 minutes, until the pecans become sugar glazed. Remove pecans from the pan and set aside. Add ½ cup of the candied pecans to the batter and gently fold in.

5. Make pancakes in large lightly oiled skillet. Turn heat to medium-high and pour in ¼ cup batter. Cook pancakes on one side until bubbles appear on surface, then turn and cook on the other side until golden brown. Serve 3 pancakes on a plate, top with a dollop of Nutella, and garnish with the remainder sugar glazed pecans. (Nutella can be heated in microwave about 5 seconds for smooth consistency.) Makes 12 large pancakes.

Time: 30 Minutes

STRAWBERRY GREEK YOGURT PARFAITS WITH WHIPPED CREAM

Note: *We were not raised eating yogurt, but I did discover that yogurt was popular and made in Puglia, Italy, so I included them in my recipes. This is an alternative for breakfast or anytime.*

1 recipe **Homemade Crunchy Granola** on next page

4 cups fresh strawberries, washed, stems removed, and sliced thick

1 tablespoon sugar

1 (32-ounce) container Chobani Greek low-fat yogurt

2 tablespoons pure honey

Whipping cream

Peppermint sprigs

1. Prepare homemade granola as directed; set aside. Place strawberries in small bowl with sugar and stir together; place in refrigerator for 15 minutes. Remove strawberries; set aside.

2. Remove yogurt from carton into a medium bowl. Add the honey and stir together with yogurt until well blended. Using 4 large parfait glasses, start with yogurt on bottom, about ⅓ cup. Next, add about ¼ cup strawberries and 1 tablespoon granola. Continue layering the glass with yogurt, strawberries, and granola until reaching the top. End with strawberries over the yogurt. Top with whipped cream and 1 tablespoon granola. Garnish each parfait with a peppermint sprig. Makes 4 parfaits.

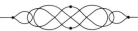
Time: 30 Minutes

HOMEMADE CRUNCHY GRANOLA

Note: *Homemade Granola is really easy to make and has many uses. Any dried fruit can be used in ½ cup measurements.*

4 cups old fashioned rolled oats

2 cups shredded coconut

1 cup brown sugar

¾ cup chopped pecans

¾ cup sliced almonds

5 tablespoons mild olive oil

6 tablespoons pure honey

½ cup raisons

½ cup dried cranberries

½ cup dried cherries

1. Preheat oven to 350 degrees. In very large bowl, combine oats, coconut, brown sugar, pecans and almonds. Stir together well.

2. Combine oil and honey in a small saucepan, and heat on stove until thin and warm. Pour over the granola mixture and coat with a large spoon, or clean hands.

3. Spread the granola over a large baking pan, 16x12-inch. Place in heated oven and bake for 20 minutes, stirring every 6 to 8 minutes. Some of the granola will begin to clump together. Remove from oven and place in large bowl. Add the raisons, cranberries, and cherries. Stir well and let cool. Store in airtight container. Makes 8 cups granola.

THE GOOD OLD DAYS

I am not sure where the days go, but here we are in early August, and I am thinking about getting the house decorated for the upcoming holidays. I figure if I can't put a stop to the days, I might as well start wrapping Christmas presents. Am I the only one who can't seem to catch up? Life just seemed to be less crazy when I was a kid growing up. For one thing, we didn't start school until after Labor Day in September. My mom never ran out and bought me a whole new wardrobe, mainly because I had two uniforms that she washed out every other day. My socks were white and my shoes were black, and as I recall, no one stood out as a fashion star. As far as my supplies, if I had two sharp pencils and a notebook, all I needed was a teacher and a desk.

However, I did need discipline, and at my school that was no problem. My mother made it clear that if I got in trouble at school, I got in trouble at home. I was expected to be courteous, kind, non-violent, and in no way disobedient to authority. If I was lucky I got to watch the Howdy Doody show when I got home, and of course my favorite, the Mickey Mouse Club. It was a kid's world with beautiful Annette Funicello and the Mouseketeers. Saturdays were heaven with the Lone Ranger, and Kukla, Fran and Ollie. Life was really simple.

We had one car, and that belonged to dad so he could get to work. He was a butcher at the local National Food Store in Jennings, Missouri where I grew up. Mom walked to work where she was a seamstress and I walked to school.

We seldom had obesity problems, because when we were not walking, we played hard on our school playground for at least an hour every day. On the way home from school, if it snowed, we ran most of the way to avoid snowballs aimed at our heads from the mean boys.

We were happy kids, had homemade meals every night, and always sat together at the supper table. We discussed the days' problems, and got very little sympathy if we had complaints. We mostly learned to work out our own problems at school, and seldom did our parents get involved. We could take piano or accordion lessons after school, or learn to play an instrument of our choice through school programs. Sundays and Wednesdays were reserved for church, and there were very few activities, if any, scheduled on these days.

We learned to cook from our moms, and our brothers worked with our dads either building something or taking it apart. Everything that broke down in our house was fixed by my dad. Keeping the house in order and somewhat cleaned was up to my mom. Since she loved to cook, the other things lacked somewhat. But did we ever have the best meals and desserts! I can still smell the hot baked bread and the wonderful Honey Pecan Rolls she would make on the weekends for our special treat.

So those were the *Good Old Days* . . . makes me feel like taking the train back home. Hopefully, we can capture some of that family time, at least a few evenings per week. Your kids will love it, even if pulls them away from their favorite video game.

Rosalie

Time: 2 Hours, 30 Minutes

HONEY PECAN BREAKFAST ROLLS

Note: *Italians love pairing honey and nuts together, and this recipe is exceptional.*
I must admit my recipe is definitely sweeter than my mom's, but then she just may love my version.
Get up early before your family does on Saturday or Sunday, and surprise them with this little bit of heaven.

1 tablespoon yeast

2 tablespoons sugar

1 cup milk, warmed to 110 degrees

2 large eggs

4 tablespoons butter, melted

2 tablespoons honey

1 teaspoon pure vanilla

3¾ cups all-purpose flour

2 teaspoons salt

2 tablespoons butter, melted

Topping

4 tablespoons butter, melted

½ cup honey

½ cup light brown sugar

½ teaspoon vanilla

1 cup pecan pieces

Filling

¼ cup butter, melted

1 cup light brown sugar

1 tablespoon cinnamon

1. Preheat oven to 350 degrees. Use sweet cream butter, not salted, in this recipe. Place yeast, sugar, and warm milk in large mixing bowl. Using blender beater, mix the yeast, sugar, and milk just until blended; let stand 5 minutes to allow the yeast to foam up. Add eggs, butter, honey, and vanilla. Beat on low speed a few seconds, just to blend to smooth consistency. Add the flour and salt, and continue to mix on low speed to bring the dough together, about 15 seconds. Remove blender beater and add dough hook attachment. Mix for 15 seconds, or knead by hand for 1 to 2 minutes to form a dough ball. Do not handle the dough too much.

2. Brush a large bowl with 2 tablespoons melted butter and add the dough, turning once to coat. Cover with light towel and let rise for 1 hour, or until doubled in size.

3. Punch dough down and let rest in bowl. Make the topping by placing the butter, honey, brown sugar, and vanilla in a small saucepan. Heat the topping until sugar and honey dissolve. Remove from stove and divide the topping among a 12-cup regular muffin pan and a 6-cup regular muffin pan. Sprinkle the pecans over the topping.

4. Place dough ball on a flour-dusted counter. Roll the dough out to a 14x18-inch rectangle, turning dough and dusting with flour to avoid sticking. Pour the ¼ cup melted butter over the dough and smear the butter over the dough with clean hand. Combine the sugar and cinnamon; mix together well. Sprinkle the cinnamon sugar over the butter. Roll the rectangle up jelly-roll style, stretching the dough roll a little as you go. Place the roll with seam-side down. Cut the roll into 16 to 18 slices. Place the dough slices over the honey topping. Cover with towel and let rise in warm place 1 hour. Bake in oven for 12 to 14 minutes, or until golden. Remove from oven and turn the rolls out. Scoop out any residual topping and drizzle over the rolls. Serve warm. Makes 16 to 18 rolls.

Time: 40 Minutes

BEST EVER SCONES WITH ALMOND GLAZE

Note: *These scones were featured in the December 2010 issue of the Southern Living magazine by Betty Joyce Mills, and they are honestly the best I have ever had. My family could not stop eating them. Serve with a strong espresso for the best!*

2 cups all-purpose flour

⅓ cup sugar

1 tablespoon baking powder

½ teaspoon salt

½ cup cold butter

1 cup heavy whipping cream, divided

¼ cup dried cranberries or cherries

Almond Glaze

1 cup powdered sugar

3 to 4 tablespoons milk

½ teaspoon almond extract

1. Preheat oven to 450 degrees. In medium bowl, combine the flour, sugar, baking powder, and salt. Cut the butter into flour mixture with a pastry blender or with clean hands until mixture is crumbly and resembles small peas. Put bowl with flour mixture in freezer for 10 minutes.

2. Remove bowl from freezer and add ¾ cup plus 2 tablespoons cream and dried fruit. Stir just until dry ingredients are moistened. Turn dough out onto a cutting board or waxed paper and pat into a 7 to 8-inch round (mixture will be crumbly.) Cut the round into 8 wedges, and gently place the wedges onto a pizza stone or lightly greased cookie sheet. Separate the wedges about 2-inches apart. Brush tops of wedges with remaining 2 tablespoons cream. Bake for 12 to 14 minutes or until golden.

3. Make the almond glaze by placing 1 cup powdered sugar in small bowl. Add the milk and almond extract; mix together until smooth. Drizzle glaze on scones and serve warm. Makes 8 Scones.

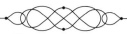

Time: 30 Minutes

PUFF PASTRY WITH MASCARPONE CHERRY FILLING

Note: *Love a puff pastry with your morning espresso? This is just the recipe! They are delicious just plain or with pie cherries.*

1 (8-ounce) carton mascarpone cheese

⅓ cup sugar

1 large egg

2 tablespoons ricotta cheese

1 teaspoon vanilla extract

1 tablespoon grated lemon zest

2 sheets (1 box) frozen puff pastry, defrosted

½ cup butter, melted and divided

1 egg

1 tablespoon water

1 can cherry pie filling, optional

Sugar crystals

1. Preheat oven to 400 degrees. Place the mascarpone cheese and sugar in a mixing bowl, and on medium speed, cream the cheese and sugar until smooth. Add the egg, ricotta, vanilla, and lemon zest; mix until smooth.

2. Unfold one sheet of puff pastry onto a lightly floured counter and roll with rolling pin to a 10x10-inch square. Cut the sheet into 4 equal squares with a sharp knife. Brush the sheet with melted butter. Place 1½ tablespoons cheese filling into the middle of each of the four squares. Beat the egg with the water to make an egg wash. Brush the border of each pastry with egg wash and fold two opposite corners to the center, brushing and overlapping the corners of each pastry to seal. If using cherries, place 1 tablespoon over the middle fold, or a dollop of cherries can be placed over the cheese before sealing pastry.

3. Cover a 15x10-inch cookie sheet with parchment paper. Place the pastries on the parchment paper and bake in oven for 16 to 18 minutes, or until puffed and brown. Remove from oven and lightly brush the warm pastries with butter. Sprinkle sugar crystals over pastries. Makes 8 pastries.

Time: 45 Minutes

BEST EVER BANANA BREAD
WITH VANILLA CREAM ICING

Note: *I am in love with this recipe, and it may be the best banana bread ever! It may not be Italian, but my family has always made it plain, with a little powdered sugar sprinkled over the top. I have to admit, I like it sweet with a good butter cream icing.*

1 tablespoon butter

1 cup sugar

½ cup butter

2 eggs

3 large ripe bananas

½ cup buttermilk

1 teaspoon vanilla

2 cups flour

1 teaspoon baking powder

1 teaspoon baking soda

1 teaspoon salt

½ cup pecans, coarsely chopped

1 tablespoon sugar

½ cup pecans, coarsely chopped, optional

1.	Preheat oven to 350 degrees. Butter a 9x5-inch baking pan. Using an electric mixer, cream sugar and butter until light and creamy. Beat in the eggs, bananas, buttermilk, and vanilla.

2.	Combine the flour, baking powder, baking soda, and salt. Stir the flour mixture into the banana mixture just until moistened.

3.	Place the pecans and sugar in small frying pan and stir together constantly until sugar is dissolved and pecans are candied, about 3 minutes. Fold the pecans into the batter and pour batter into prepared pan. Bake for 30 to 35 minutes, or until toothpick comes out dry. Let cool and top with vanilla cream icing.

Vanilla Cream Icing

4 tablespoons butter

2 cups powdered sugar

4 to 5 tablespoons half-and-half

1 teaspoon vanilla extract

Cream butter and powdered sugar until combined; mixture will be thick. Add the half-and-half, and continue to beat until smooth; add more half-and-half if icing too thick. Add the vanilla and continue to stir until smooth and creamy; spread over the banana bread. Sprinkle with pecans pieces if desired. Serves 12.

Ross David & Gia

SOUPS & SALADS

One of the most comforting foods known to man is a bowl of soup. This fact goes back to Bible days when even Esau, tired and hungry, traded his birthright for a bowl of lentil soup. It is the one thing that seems to calm us, cheer us, and even at times, cure our colds. How many times have we gone out to a restaurant and, out of all the items on the menu, still choose soup and salad? Maybe it's the magic in the hot soup that lifts our spirits. And since salads can be meals in themselves, our palate is pleased and our soul is fed.

Italians love soup, and are noted for making some of the most popular of soups. It is also common in the Italian cuisine to add dumplings and/or pastas to the broth, giving the soup a hearty character. Take the awesome Chicken Gnocchi Soup, and of course the ever popular Pasta é Fagioli soup, featuring acini de pepe pasta. Both are commonly ordered on Italian menus, and enjoyed along with wonderful Italian salads.

The salads in this section can be as simple as Bibb Lettuce with Olive Oil/ Lemon Dressing to the hearty Antipasta Salad with Honey Vinaigrette. So, dip up a bowl of yummy soup, and make a salad to go along. You will totally love this section. My suggestions follow:

1. If you are using a small amount of noodles, or quick-cooking pasta, add it directly to the soup at the end of cooking. If using the dumplings, as in the Chicken Gnocchi Soup, boil the dumplings for half the time, then add to the soup to complete cooking.

2. When adding a stock to the soup, always use Kitchen Basics brand. It is my favorite, and by far the best stock.

3. Soups freeze well in quart or gallon freezer bags, and are a welcome meal when pressed for time.

4. Soups go well with a hot loaf of Italian bread. Be sure to have a loaf on hand when making soup. Dipping the bread in the hot soup makes it more delicious.

5. Love salads? Be creative and try all sorts of fresh greens. Arugula is a peppery green and adds a bite to the salad. Darker greens such as red leaf and spinach are a wonderful mix to baby greens, radicchio, and even escarole.

6. The essentials for a great salad are four things: A good extra virgin olive oil, Balsamic or red wine vinegar, coarse sea salt, and of course fresh ground black pepper. Other additives are welcome, such as fresh lemon juice, honey, and Italian spices.

7. Don't dress the salad with the Italian dressing too far in advance of serving the salad. The vinegar and salt will wilt the salad.

Italian Beef Soup with Meatballs
on page 62

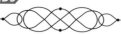
Time: 1½ Hours

CABBAGE LENTIL SOUP

Note: *Italians love lentils, and this soup is full of good flavor plus nutrition. It is made with lean pork to give it a savory flavor and lots of vegetables for a full-bodied soup. To make it just a vegetable soup, omit the meat.*

1 to 2 lean bone-in pork chops

Lawry's coarse garlic salt
with parsley added

3 tablespoons olive oil, divided

1 large onion, quartered small

2 cloves garlic, chopped small

1 medium potato, quartered small

3 stalks celery, chopped medium

3 carrots, cleaned and chopped small

1 teaspoon salt

½ teaspoon pepper

½ to 1 cup water

1 (15-ounce) can diced tomatoes

1 (29-ounce) can tomato sauce

1 tablespoon beef base, or 2 to 3 beef
bouillon cubes

1 (15-ounce) can green beans, drained

1 large head cabbage, cored and
chopped in chunks

1 quart container Kitchen Basics
Beef Stock

1 cup dried lentils

4 cups baby spinach, washed,
and stems removed

1. Trim all fat from pork chops and sprinkle liberally with the garlic salt. Pour 2 tablespoons olive oil into a skillet and fry the pork chops until golden on both sides. Remove chops and set aside. (If only using vegetables, begin with the vegetables and 2 tablespoons olive oil.)

2. In a large 8-quart heavy pot, add the onion and garlic and another tablespoon olive oil. Sauté the onion and garlic for 2 to 3 minutes. Add the potato, celery, and carrots and sprinkle the vegetables with salt and pepper. Let the vegetables cook about 6 to 8 minutes. Add ½ cup water or more to loosen vegetables.

3. Add the tomatoes, tomato sauce, and beef base. Next, add the green beans, cabbage, and beef stock. Stir the soup well. Now add the lentils and the prepared pork chops. Stir again, and let the soup cook on medium-low heat for 1 hour or until cabbage and lentils are tender.

4. Before serving, add the spinach, and let the soup cook for about another 6 to 8 minutes to wilt the spinach. Remove bones from pork chops and dice the meat. Add the diced meat back to the soup, and stir well. Ladle the soup into soup bowls, and serve hot. Makes 12 servings.

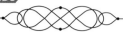

Time: 1 Hour

PASTA É FAGIOLI SOUP

Note: *Pasta é Fagioli is a delicious classic Italian soup and can be found at most Italian restaurants. You will love this version, and the whole family will love you for making it. Serve with your favorite crusty Italian bread.*

⅓ cup extra virgin olive oil

1 medium onion, chopped

2 cloves garlic, chopped

⅔ cup celery, chopped small

½ cup carrots, chopped small

1 pound ground mild Italian sausage

1 (28-ounce) can diced tomatoes, juice included

1 (15-ounce) can cannellini beans, drained

1 (15-ounce) can red kidney beans, drained

2 teaspoons oregano

1 teaspoon salt

¼ teaspoon ground black pepper

¼ teaspoon crushed red pepper flakes

2 tablespoons curly parsley, chopped

1½ cups Kitchen Basics chicken stock

1 (15-ounce) can tomato sauce

¾ cup ditali pasta

2 teaspoons salt

1 cup reserved pasta water

Parmesan cheese

1.   Pour olive oil into an 8-quart sauce pan, and sauté onion, garlic, celery, and carrots for 8 to 10 minutes. Add the ground sausage, and continue to fry with the vegetables another 8 to 10 minutes, until meat is no longer pink.

2.   Add the tomatoes, cannellini beans, red kidney beans, oregano, salt, pepper, red pepper flakes, and parsley. Stir the soup well and simmer 5 to 10 minutes. Add the chicken stock and tomato sauce. Stir well and let simmer with lid on for 15 minutes. Remove lid and stir soup. Taste, and add additional salt and pepper if desired.

3.   Boil the ditali pasta in salted water for 3 to 4 minutes. Drain pasta, reserving 1 cup pasta water; add the undercooked pasta directly to the soup. Continue to cook for another 5 minutes for pasta to be al dente. If soup feels too thick, add some or all of the reserved pasta water. Serve in pasta bowls and garnish with plenty of Parmesan cheese. Serves 6.

Time: 30 Minutes

ZUPPA TOSCANA

Note: *This classic soup is served in many Italian restaurants and is a favorite no matter what the occasion. It is a potato/sausage soup with a savory chicken stock.*

1 pound ground Italian sausage, mild or spicy

1 teaspoon red pepper flakes

3 slices bacon, optional

2 tablespoons olive oil

1 large onion, chopped small

2 cloves garlic, chopped fine

1 (32-ounce) box Kitchen Basics chicken stock

1 quart water

2 to 3 chicken bouillon cubes

2 large baking potatoes

1 cup heavy cream

2 cups fresh kale, chopped small

Parmesan cheese

Ground black pepper

1. Fry sausage in large soup pot or Dutch oven over medium heat until sausage is no longer pink, about 10 minutes. Remove from pan and drain grease; break sausage into small pieces and set aside. Sprinkle red pepper flakes over sausage.

2. Fry bacon if using, in same pot until bacon is crisp; remove bacon and discard grease. Crumble bacon and add to sausage; set aside.

3. Pour olive oil into pot and add the onion and garlic; stir-fry until onion is soft, about 5 to 6 minutes. Add the sausage and bacon back to the pot with the onions. Add the chicken stock, water, and bouillon cubes. Bring soup to gentle boil.

4. Wash potatoes and leave skins on. Cut potatoes down the middle, lengthwise, and slice the potatoes into ¼-inch slices on cutting board. Add all of the potatoes to the soup pot, and cook over medium heat until the potatoes are soft, about 20 minutes. When potatoes are tender, add the cream and stir well; let soup simmer on low until the cream is heated through. Add kale and let soup continue to cook until kale is soft. Pour the soup into soup bowls and garnish with fresh grated Parmesan cheese and fresh ground black pepper. Serve with a hard roll. Serves 8.

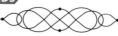
Time: 1 Hour and 15 Minutes

ITALIAN WEDDING SOUP

Note: *This soup is very popular in Italian-American restaurants, and I can only describe it as "simply delicious." The name possibly came from the marriage of "meat and greens" and how well the meatballs and greens pair together.*

5 quarts water

1 whole soup chicken

3 stalks celery with leaves, cut in halves

2 medium carrots, peeled and halved

1 medium onion, halved

2 to 3 sprigs fresh parsley

1 tablespoon salt

¼ teaspoon ground black pepper

1 pound ground chuck or sirloin

¼ cup plain bread crumbs

¼ cup grated Parmesan cheese

1 clove garlic, chopped fine

2 tablespoon fresh curly parsley

2 eggs

1 teaspoon salt

⅛ teaspoon ground black pepper

1 head escarole, chopped, about 4 cups

½ pound acini di pepe pasta

Coarse ground black pepper

Freshly grated Parmesan cheese

1. Using an 8-quart pot, add 5 quarts water. Rinse chicken under cool water, and remove liver, gizzard, and neck; use for later, or discard. Place chicken in pot with water. Add the celery, carrots, onion, parsley, salt, and pepper. Bring to boil and skim foam as it rises to the top. Cover with lid and cook for 1 hour or longer, until the chicken is tender.

2. Remove chicken to platter and let cool completely. Remove vegetables from broth and discard, or if desired, leave a few of the vegetables. Bring broth to soft boil and make meatballs by combining ground chuck, bread crumbs, cheese, garlic, parsley, eggs, salt, and pepper. Mix together well and make tiny meatballs, about the size of large grapes. Drop the meatballs into the hot broth; skim any foam from meatballs as it rises to top and remove. Skin and debone the cooled chicken; cut into small pieces and return to broth. Let the meatballs and chicken cook together about 10 minutes.

3. Rinse the escarole and remove bottom core; chop and add to the broth. Keep broth on soft boil and simmer for 5 minutes. Add the acini di pepe directly to the soup; simmer an additional 10 to 12 minutes. Add the pepper as desired. This soup will have a rich chicken and beef flavor. Ladle soup into soup bowls and garnish with freshly grated Parmesan cheese. Serves 8 to 10.

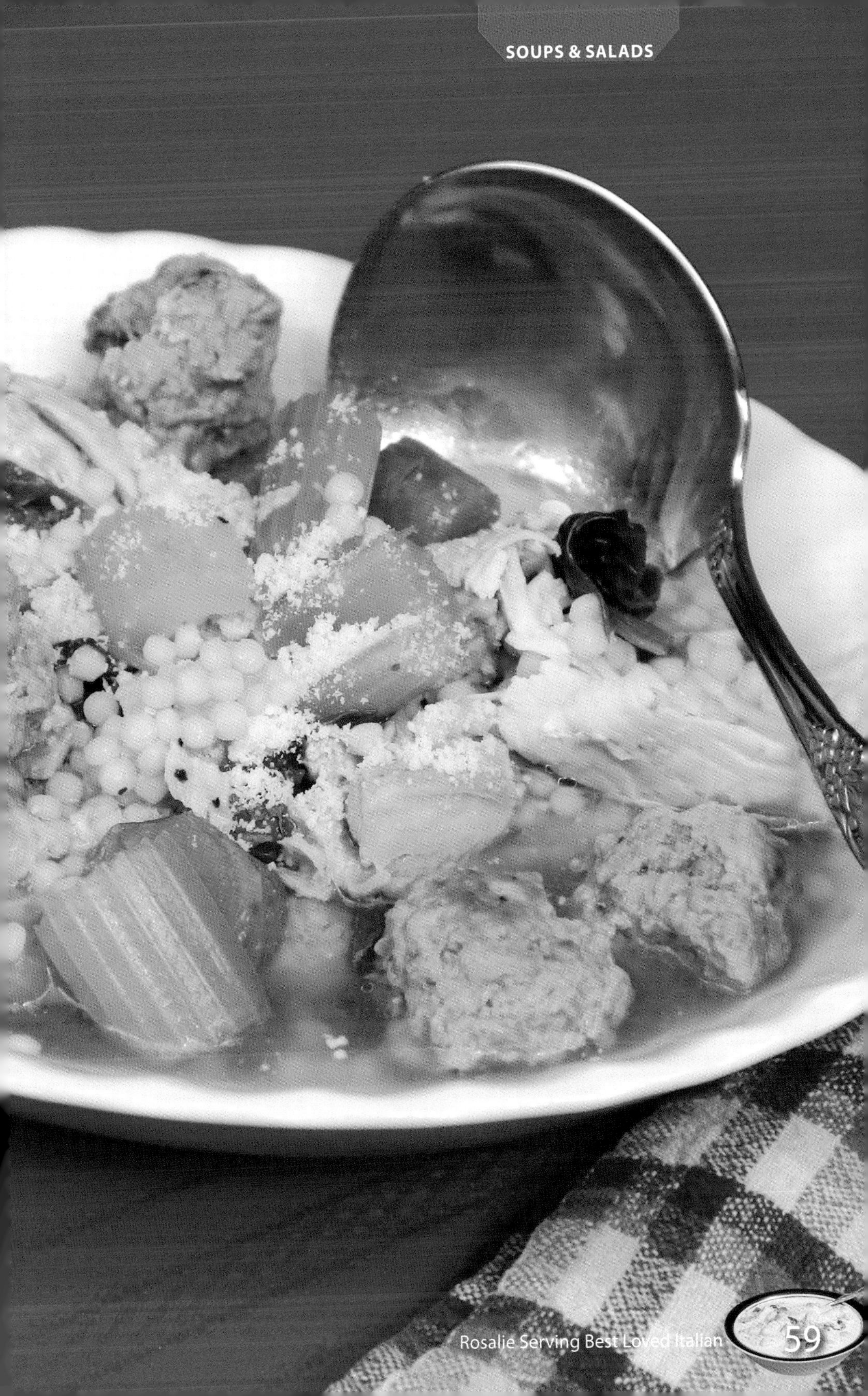

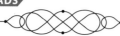
Time: 1 Hour And 15 Minutes

MINESTRONE

Note: *This soup has been served on Italian tables for a long time, and is still a favorite pick in Italian restaurants.*

4 ounces pancetta, chopped, about ½ cup

3 tablespoons olive oil

1 medium onion, small quartered

2 cloves garlic, chopped

2 cups celery, chopped into 1-inch pieces

1 cup carrots, peeled and chopped into 1-inch pieces

1 cup potatoes, unpeeled and small quartered

4 cups cabbage, chopped into small pieces

1 teaspoon salt

¼ teaspoon ground black pepper

1 (28-ounce) can diced tomatoes, juice included

6 cups Kitchen Basics chicken stock

2 cans cannellini beans, drained and rinsed

1 bay leaf

2 tablespoons fresh curly parsley

½ teaspoon crushed red pepper flakes

½ teaspoon dried basil

1 teaspoon salt

¼ teaspoon ground black pepper

1 small tender zucchini, unpeeled and chopped small

½ cup ditali pasta

Extra water, if needed

Parmesan cheese

1. Pour olive oil into large skillet and fry the pancetta 3 to 4 minutes, turning often. Add the onion and garlic and sauté together about 5 minutes. Add the celery, carrot, and potatoes; continue to stir-fry for a few more minutes. Add the cabbage, salt, and pepper. Continue frying another 5 to 6 minutes until the vegetables become crisp-tender. Add the tomatoes and cook until heated through, another 5 minutes.

2. Transfer the vegetables to an 8-quart pot. Add the chicken stock, beans, bay leaf, parsley, crushed red pepper flakes, basil, salt, and pepper. Bring soup to a soft boil and let simmer for about 40 minutes. The vegetables should be soft, but not mushy.

3. Add the zucchini and pasta together. Cook for an additional 7 minutes. Add additional water if soup is too thick, starting with a half cup at a time. Taste, and add any additional seasoning as desired. Ladle soup into small pasta bowls and garnish with freshly grated Parmesan cheese. Serves 8.

Time: 30 Minutes

CHICKEN GNOCCHI SOUP
(POTATO DUMPLINGS)

Note: *This soup is creamy and rich with tender chicken, gnocchi dumplings, and lots of Parmesan cheese. You will serve this often and it may become a family tradition.*

2 skinless chicken breasts, cut into small pieces, about 2 cups

Lawry's coarse garlic salt

Olive oil

¼ cup extra virgin olive oil

2 tablespoons butter

½ cup shredded carrots

½ cup celery, chopped small

2 cloves garlic, chopped fine

1 cup Kitchen Basics chicken stock

1 quart heavy whipping cream

3 cups Parmesan cheese

Coarse ground black pepper

1 pound gnocchi dumplings

1 tablespoon salt

2 cups fresh baby spinach leaves

1. Rinse chicken breasts in cool water; pat dry. Sprinkle lightly with garlic salt on both sides. Using cutting board, cut breasts into small pieces. Place in large skillet and brown chicken in olive oil until no longer pink, about 2 to 3 minutes.

2. Using same skillet, move chicken to side of pan and add olive oil and butter. Sauté carrots, celery and garlic until crisp tender, about 4 to 5 minutes. Add the chicken stock and let simmer about 2 minutes.

3. Add the cream and stir well. Add the cheese, one cup at a time, stirring constantly until cheese is melted into the cream. Add the coarse ground black pepper to taste.

4. Parboil the gnocchi in salted boiling water for 2 to 3 minutes; drain and add to the soup. Let the soup simmer with the dumplings for about 4 to 5 minutes, just until dumplings are tender but not mushy. Add the spinach last, folding it into the soup just until tender. Pour soup into desired bowls. Serves 6.

Time: 1 Hour and 30 Minutes

ITALIAN BEEF SOUP WITH MEATBALLS

Note: *My mother, Ann Fiorino, would make this soup almost every week in the winter. We always looked forward to dipping her home-made Italian bread into the hot broth and savoring the little meatballs. See photo on page 51.*

½ pound stew meat, cut into 1-inch cubes

Salt and pepper

¼ cup olive oil

2 (32 ounce) cartons Kitchen Basics beef stock

2 to 3 cups water, divided

1 pound ground chuck

¼ cup plain, or Italian bread crumbs

¼ cup grated Parmesan cheese

¼ cup onion, finely chopped

2 tablespoons fresh parsley, chopped

½ teaspoon fennel seed

2 eggs

1 teaspoon salt

¼ teaspoon ground black pepper

2 cups celery with leaves, chopped 1-inch pieces

1 cup baby carrots

1 small onion, quartered small

1 to 2 medium potatoes, unpeeled, quartered small

1 (15-ounce) can diced tomatoes

1 (8-ounce) can tomato sauce

2 beef bouillon cubes, optional

½ cup acini di pepe pasta

Parmesan cheese, optional

1. Rinse stew meat in cool water; pat dry. Using kitchen scissors, cut meat into 1-inch cubes. Salt and pepper meat and place into large soup pot. Add olive oil and sauté on medium high until browned. Add the beef stock and 2 cups water; bring to gentle boil and cook for 10 minutes.

2. Prepare meatballs by placing ground chuck into a medium bowl. Add the bread crumbs, cheese, onion, parsley, fennel seed, eggs, salt, and pepper; mix well with clean hands. Form into small meatballs and add to the stew meat and beef stock. Simmer together until boiling. Skim foam from meatballs as it rises to the top.

3. Add the celery, carrots, onion, potatoes, tomatoes, and tomato sauce. Cover pot and simmer on medium heat for about 45 minutes, or until the vegetables are tender. Add remaining cup of water and beef bouillon cubes if desired; bring soup back to boil. Add the acini di pepe pasta directly to the soup; simmer an additional 10 to 12 minutes. Taste soup and add additional salt or pepper if desired. Ladle soup into soup bowls and garnish with Parmesan cheese. Serve with crusty Italian bread. Serves 6 to 8.

GAZPACHO

Note: *This is a wonderful summertime cold soup that reminds me of a chopped up Italian salad. My aunt Irene Campise would combine tomatoes, cucumbers, onions, vinegar, and oil, then dip hard Italian bread into the soup. It was so good!*

2 large red bell peppers

1 large cucumber, ends trimmed and seeds removed

4 Roma tomatoes
   or 2 medium beef steak tomatoes,
   cored and skins removed

1 medium red onion

1 tender celery stalk with leaves

3 cloves garlic, chopped fine

3 cups tomato juice

¼ cup apple cider vinegar

¼ cup extra virgin olive oil

½ teaspoon coarse sea salt

½ teaspoon ground black pepper

⅛ teaspoon crushed red pepper flakes

Pepperoncinis, optional

1 loaf crusty Italian bread

1. Core peppers and remove seeds. Chop the red bell peppers into chunks and place into a food processor and process 4 to 5 seconds, leaving the peppers finely chopped. Place the chopped peppers with its juice into a large clear bowl. Peel the cucumber and place in chopper, pulsing until the cucumber is finely chopped. Follow the same with the tomatoes, onion and celery, processing one vegetable at a time, leaving the vegetables coarsely chopped. Add the finely chopped garlic and toss with the vegetables.

2. Add the tomato juice, vinegar, olive oil, salt, pepper, and crushed red pepper flakes. Toss the soup well and place in the refrigerator to chill for a few minutes if desired, or serve immediately. Break the bread into chunks, and toast in the oven for 5 to 6 minutes. Serve with the soup. Garnish with pepperoncinis if desired. Serves 4 to 6. (Tomato juice can be made in the food processor by adding 3 large tomatoes, cored and skins removed. Run the tomatoes through a strainer to make 3 cups.)

Time: 15 Minutes

ANTIPASTA SALAD
WITH HONEY VINAIGRETTE

Note: *This salad is so delicious and full, you could make it a meal, especially if served in medium-sized Italian bread bowls. Ask for a chunk of Genoa salami from the deli, and cube it small. It is served with a sweet vinaigrette that bathes the salad with flavor.*

2 cups romaine lettuce, chopped

2 cups Bibb lettuce, chopped

2 cups iceberg lettuce, chopped

½ cup celery, chopped into 1-inch pieces

½ cup green onions, chopped small

½ can red kidney beans,
  drained and rinsed

½ cup garbanzo beans,
  drained and rinsed

¾ cup Genoa salami, cut into
  small cubes

1 cup shredded mozzarella cheese

1 large summer tomato, chopped into
  quarters or 1 cup cherry tomatoes

½ cup marinated artichoke hearts

6 pepperoncini

Honey Vinaigrette Dressing

¼ cup red wine vinegar

1 tablespoon freshly squeezed
  lemon juice

1 teaspoon honey

¾ cup extra virgin olive oil

1 teaspoon coarse sea salt

½ teaspoon coarse ground pepper

¼ teaspoon crushed red pepper flakes

1. Rinse all the lettuce and pat dry with paper towel. Place the romaine, Bibb, and iceberg lettuce into a large bowl; add the celery and green onions. Add the kidney beans, garbanzo beans, Genoa salami, and mozzarella cheese; toss the salad well.

2. Add the tomatoes and artichoke hearts and toss again. Separate the salad into 6 salad bowls, or hallowed out bread bowls; garnish each salad with a pepperoncini.

3. Make the honey vinaigrette by placing the vinegar, lemon juice, and honey into a jar with a lid. Shake together until well blended. Add the olive oil, salt, pepper, and red pepper flakes. Shake again until smooth. Pour over the salads. Makes 8 salads.

Time: 15 Minutes

Bibb Lettuce with Olive Oil/Lemon Dressing

Note: *These little Bibb lettuce bowls hold just enough salad for one serving. This salad is very beautiful all on its own, featuring only green onions and a delicious lemon dressing. Bibb lettuce is sweet and tender with a buttery texture*

6 Bibb lettuce heads

12 green onions, ends trimmed

Olive Oil/Lemon Dressing

⅔ cup extra virgin olive oil

1 teaspoon lemon zest

Juice of 2 lemons

1 teaspoon coarse sea salt

½ teaspoon freshly ground black pepper

1. Arrange lettuce heads in 6 individual bowls. Spread the leaves slightly apart. Plant 2 green onions into each of the lettuce heads.

2. Prepare the lemon dressing by pouring the olive oil into a medium jar. Add the lemon zest, juice of 2 lemons, salt, and pepper. Put lid on jar and shake dressing until well combined. Serve the dressing over the Bibb lettuce heads. Serve with crusty Italian bread. Makes 6 salads.

Time: 15 Minutes

PANZANELLA SALAD
WITH BALSAMIC VINAIGRETTE

Note: *This salad is traditionally made with hard Italian bread, extra virgin olive oil, and vinegar mixed with a little water to extend the liquid. I have paired it with a balsamic vinaigrette dressing that makes enough to soak the bread, making it a salad of wonderful flavor with every bite. Other versions include adding purple onions, fresh basil, and cucumber with a stiff-type lettuce, such as romaine.*

1 small loaf Italian or French bread, preferably 2 to 3 days old

½ cup extra virgin olive oil

Lawry's coarse garlic salt with dried parsley

4 cups romaine lettuce, washed and chopped small

2 large fresh garden tomatoes, small quartered

1 small cucumber, skin on, sliced thin

½ medium red onion, sliced into rings

1 cup fresh basil leaves

½ pound fresh buffalo mozzarella, drained and cut into 1-inch cubes

Balsamic Vinaigrette

¾ cup extra virgin olive oil

¼ cup red wine vinegar

1 tablespoon Balsamic vinegar

1 teaspoon coarse sea salt

½ teaspoon coarse black pepper

1. Preheat oven to 375 degrees. Place bread on cutting board, and cut into 1-inch slices. Cut slices into 1 to 2-inch cubes, about 5 cups. Place olive oil in large bowl; add bread cubes and stir to coat. Sprinkle bread cubes lightly with garlic salt. Spread bread cubes on large cookie sheet and sprinkle with a little more olive oil if some cubes are not coated. Place cookie sheet in oven and bake until toasted and golden brown, about 10 to 12 minutes, stirring often for even browning. Remove from oven and let sit for about 15 minutes.

2. In large bowl, place the romaine, tomatoes, cucumber, red onion, basil leaves, and 1 cup buffalo mozzarella. Add about ¾ of the toasted bread cubes, saving a portion for the top of the salad.

3. Make the balsamic vinaigrette by combining the olive oil, vinegars, salt, and pepper in a jar with a lid. Shake the ingredients well to combine. Pour dressing over the salad and toss well. Add the remaining bread cubes to top the salad. Place the salad in a large trifle bowl for a beautiful display. Serves 10.

Time: 20 Minutes

TUNA STUFFED TOMATOES

Note: *If you love fresh tomatoes and tuna, you will love these little salads.
They are so good in the summer when the fresh tomatoes are in.*

4 large fresh firm tomatoes

2 cans tuna packed in olive oil

½ cup tender celery hearts,
  chopped small

¼ cup green onions, tops included and
  chopped small

2 large boiled eggs, chopped

¼ cup green olives with pimento

⅓ cup fresh basil leaves, chopped

1 teaspoon red wine vinegar

Green curly large lettuce leaves

Peppermint sprigs

1. Cut tops off tomatoes crosswise, about ½-inch down. Gently scoop out inside of tomato, leaving side and bottom margin to support filling. Put the scooped out tomatoes in a large bowl; set aside. Pour the tuna with oil in bowl with tomatoes. Add the celery, onions, eggs, olives, basil leaves, and vinegar. Toss together gently with a fork.

2. Stuff each tomato with the filling to a little over the top. Place a large green curly lettuce leaf on 4 plates. Set the tomatoes on each of the lettuce leaves. Garnish with a small sprig of peppermint. Makes 4 salads.

Time: 10 Minutes

ROSALIE'S ITALIAN SALAD WITH BALSAMIC VINAIGRETTE

Note: *I grew up with this salad on our table almost every meal, and I can tell you, it is still as popular as ever! You can add any combination of greens, cheeses, or even croutons.*

1 bunch green leaf lettuce

1 large bunch red leaf lettuce

½ cup olives, black, green,
   or Kalamata, pitted

½ cup tender celery hearts, chopped

1 cup marinated artichokes or marinated
   artichoke salad

1 small purple onion, sliced into rings

1 large, or 2 medium tomatoes,
   vine ripened and cut into wedges

10 to 12 pepperoncinis

Balsamic Vinaigrette

¾ cup extra virgin olive oil

¼ cup red wine vinegar

1 tablespoon balsamic vinegar

1 teaspoon coarse sea salt

½ teaspoon coarse ground black pepper

2 cups rope Provel cheese
   or shredded Provolone

1. Rinse lettuce well and pat dry. Chop the lettuce coarsely and place into a large salad bowl. Add the olives, celery, artichokes, and onion rings; toss again to combine.

2. Arrange the salad into salad bowls. Place 4 tomato wedges around the salad and top the salad with 2 pepperoncinis.

3. Make the dressing by combining the olive oil, vinegars, salt, and pepper into a jar with a lid. Shake the ingredients well to combine. Pour the dressing over the salads. Top each salad with the Provolone cheese. Makes 6 to 8 salads.

GARDEN PASTA SALAD
WITH BALSAMIC VINAIGRETTE

Note: *You will love this salad for all your summer events, it is truly addictive!*

2 cups broccoli florets

2 cups cauliflower florets

½ cup green onions chopped small, tops included

½ cup black olives

½ cup red bell pepper, chopped small

3 to 4 pepperoncini, chopped small

1 large fresh garden tomato, chopped into small quarters
   or 1 (16-ounce) carton grape tomatoes, left whole

5 to 6 fresh basil leaves, torn small

1 clove garlic, minced

Balsamic Vinaigrette

¾ cup extra virgin olive oil

¼ cup red wine vinegar

1 tablespoon balsamic vinegar

1 teaspoon coarse sea salt

½ teaspoon coarse black pepper

1 (12-ounce) package Barilla
   tri-color rotini

1 tablespoon salt

Basil sprigs

1. Rinse broccoli and cauliflower in cool water. Break broccoli and cauliflower into small florets, removing hard stems and core; place into large bowl.

2. Place green onions, black olives, red bell pepper, pepperoncini, tomato, basil leaves, and garlic into bowl with broccoli and cauliflower. Make the balsamic vinaigrette by placing the olive oil, vinegars, salt, and pepper into a jar with lid. Shake jar well and pour over the vegetables; marinate 15 minutes.

3. Boil rotini in salted water for 7 minutes, drain well and do not rinse pasta with water. Place warm rotini in bowl with vegetables and vinaigrette; stir well to coat pasta with dressing. Serve in small 1-cup bowls and garnish each bowl with a basil sprig. Makes 12 servings.

Time: 30 Minutes

SICILIAN GREEN BEAN SALAD WITH CIDER VINEGAR DRESSING

Note: *This could be one of the most popular of Sicilian summer salads. I love it when the green beans and potatoes are still warm.*

2 pounds fresh green beans,
  ends trimmed and left whole

5 to 6 new potatoes, unpeeled
  and small quartered

2 teaspoons salt

1 large yellow onion, sliced thin

2 cloves garlic, minced

2 large fresh vine-ripened tomatoes,
  cored and quartered

Cider Vinegar Dressing

½ cup extra virgin olive oil

¼ cup cider vinegar

1 teaspoon coarse sea salt

¼ teaspoon freshly ground black pepper

1. Rinse green beans and potatoes and place in large pot with water to barely cover green beans; add salt and bring to boil. Cook the green beans and potatoes together until tender, about 15 to 20 minutes. Drain green beans and potatoes and transfer to large bowl. While still warm, add the onions, garlic, and tomatoes.

2. Make the cider vinegar dressing by combining the olive oil, vinegar, salt and pepper; put in jar with lid and shake well. Pour the dressing over the salad and toss together. Makes 4 to 6 servings.

Time: 30 Minutes

CELEBRATION CHICKEN SALAD

Note: *This beautiful salad is very light and creamy and, served on a bed of spring greens, everyone can have their own. I made it Italian because of the purple grapes, pecans, and mixed greens.*

2 fresh bone-in chicken breasts

1 tablespoon chicken base
  or 2 chicken bouillon cubes

¾ cup celery, chopped small

¼ cup onion, chopped small

1 cup purple seedless grapes, whole

1 cup pecans, whole

1 cup mayonnaise

¼ cup sour cream

1 tablespoon lemon juice

1 teaspoon sugar

Large bag of spring mix greens,
  or greens of choice

Cluster of purple grapes

1. Rinse chicken breasts in cool water, remove skin and fat. Place breasts in heavy 4-quart pot; cover with water and add the chicken base. Bring to boil and remove any foam as it rises to the top. Cover, and let cook until breasts are tender, about 25 minutes. Remove to cool completely; cut into very small pieces.

2. Place the chicken in a large bowl; add the celery, onion, grapes, and pecans. Toss together well.

3. Make the dressing by combining mayonnaise, sour cream, lemon juice, and sugar. Add to chicken mixture and mix together well. Prepare small salad plates by placing about 1 cup greens on each plate. Place scoop of the chicken salad over the greens. Garnish with cluster of grapes on platter for accent. Makes 8 servings.

Time: 20 Minutes

SALMON SPINACH SALAD

Note: *This dish is so delicious and it can be a meal in itself. If you love baked salmon, you will love this dish*

4 salmon filets, 1½-inch thick

¼ cup butter

¼ cup extra virgin olive oil

2 tablespoons freshly squeezed lemon juice

1 teaspoon Lawry's coarse garlic salt with parsley added

Olive oil

1 (10-ounce) package fresh spinach, stems removed

1 cup walnuts, divided

1 cup sun-dried tomatoes, divided

1 cup fresh tomatoes, quartered and divided

2 cups rope Provel cheese, or shredded provolone cheese

1 cup white capped mushrooms, thick-sliced, divided

Balsamic Vinaigrette

¾ cup extra virgin olive oil

¼ cup red wine vinegar

1 tablespoon balsamic vinegar

1 teaspoon coarse sea salt

½ teaspoon freshly ground coarse black pepper

2 lemon slices

1. Preheat oven to 475 degrees. Mix butter, olive oil, lemon juice, and garlic salt in a jar with lid. Shake well to blend. Coat a foiled-covered cookie sheet with olive oil. Lay the salmon filets on the foil. Pierce each fillet with a fork in several places. Pour the olive oil/butter mixture evenly over the filets. Place baking sheet in oven and roast the filets uncovered about 10 to 12 minutes, or until the salmon is pink and flakes easily. Remove from oven and lift salmon away from the thick bottom skin with a flat turner and discard; place salmon back on baking pan. Spoon pan juices over the filets.

2. In four large salad bowls, divide the spinach. Divide the walnuts, sun dried tomatoes, fresh tomatoes, Provel cheese, and mushrooms among the spinach bowls.

3. Make the dressing by placing the olive oil, vinegars, salt, and pepper in a jar with lid. Shake the dressing to blend. Pour the dressing over each of the salads. Lay a salmon filet over the center of each salad and garnish with lemon slices. Makes 4 large salads.

Time: 15 Minutes

BROCCOLI & CAULIFLOWER SALAD

Note: *This is a great salad for any occasion, and complements most any entrée.*

2 cups broccoli florets

2 cups cauliflower florets

⅓ cup green onions, chopped small, tops included

½ cup celery, chopped small, leaves included

¼ cup Spanish olives with pimento

⅓ cup Genoa salami, small cubed

¾ cup extra virgin olive oil

¼ cup red wine vinegar

1 tablespoon balsamic vinegar

1 teaspoon coarse sea salt

½ teaspoon coarse ground black pepper

Red curly lettuce leaves

In large bowl, combine the broccoli, cauliflower, green onions, celery, olives, and Genoa salami; toss together. Make the dressing by placing the olive oil, vinegars, salt and pepper in a jar with a lid. Shake the dressing to combine and pour over the salad. Serve in individual plates over a large red curly lettuce leaf. Makes 6 salads.

Time: 15 Minutes

BROCCOLI SALAD WITH
PROVOLONE & PROSCIUTTO

Note: Prosciutto is an Italian ham that is cured with salt and spices, and it gives this dish a real punch.
Paired with the creamy dressing, it is sure to excite your taste buds.

12 slices prosciutto

2 heads broccoli

1 (8- ounce) bag shredded provolone
or rope provolone, if available

5 green onions cut small, tops included

1 (16-ounce) carton cherry tomatoes

1¼ cup mayonnaise

½ cup sugar

1 teaspoon lemon juice

3 tablespoons cider vinegar

Curly red lettuce leaves

1. Cut the prosciutto into small pieces; set aside.

2. Rinse broccoli in cool water; pat dry. Trim stems from broccoli and separate into small florets. Place florets in large bowl. Add prosciutto, provolone, onions, and tomatoes.

3. In small bowl, combine mayonnaise, sugar, lemon juice, and vinegar. Mix well and add to broccoli mixture, stirring and coating the vegetables evenly. Serve on small salad plates over large curly red lettuce leaves. Serves 12.

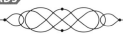

Time: 10 Minutes

CAPRESE SALAD

Note: *Insalata Caprese comes from the Isle of Capri and is one of the most popular of Italian summer salads. If possible, use only vine-ripened tomatoes and fresh grown basil for the best flavor.*

½ pound buffalo mozzarella cheese, drained
   and sliced ¼-inch, then quartered

2 large fresh vine-ripened tomatoes, small quartered
   or 1 cup cherry tomatoes, halved

1 cup fresh basil leaves, torn in pieces

⅓ cup extra virgin olive oil

2 tablespoons freshly squeezed lemon juice

1 teaspoon coarse sea salt

¼ teaspoon freshly ground black pepper

Place the mozzarella, tomatoes, and basil leaves in a medium bowl. Whisk together the olive oil, lemon juice, salt, and pepper. Pour dressing over salad and toss. Serve with toasted Italian bread. Serves 4.

GARLIC GRILLED CHICKEN OVER SPRING GREENS & RASPBERRY POPPY SEED VINAIGRETTE

Note: *This salad is my way of ushering in the beautiful season of spring. The grilled chicken is tangy and warm and when laid over baby spring greens; it is complemented by fruit, Feta, and a delightful dressing. Served with your favorite crusty bread, it is a meal.*

2 pounds chicken, preferably 12 tenderloins

Lawry's coarse garlic salt with parsley

Olive oil

1 (8-ounce) package spring greens

3 cups romaine lettuce, chopped

½ cup red onion, chopped small

1 cup celery, chopped medium

2 cups red raspberries

1 cup blueberries

1 large red apple, sliced

1 cup pecans

1 tablespoon sugar

2 (5-ounce) containers Feta cheese, about 1¼ cups

Raspberry Poppy Seed Vinaigrette

⅓ cup extra virgin olive oil

6 tablespoons red wine vinegar

1 teaspoon honey

⅔ cup red raspberry preserves

1 tablespoon warm water, optional

1 teaspoon poppy seeds

1 teaspoon coarse sea salt

¼ teaspoon ground black pepper

1. Wash and rinse chicken tenderloins. Sprinkle tenderloins with the garlic salt and coat each side in olive oil. Grill the tenderloins about 6 to 8 minutes on each side. Remove and set aside for 5 to 10 minutes while preparing the salad. Tenderloins can be pan-fried if no grill available.

2. Place salad greens, romaine, onion, and celery in a large bowl; set aside. In another bowl add the raspberries, blueberries, and apple; toss together. Place the pecans in a dry skillet with sugar added and over medium low heat, stir the pecans until candied, or until the sugar disappears, about 2 to 3 minutes. Add the pecans to the fruit mixture. Add the fruit mixture to the salad greens and toss together.

3. Make the raspberry poppy seed vinaigrette by combining the olive oil, vinegar, honey, raspberry preserves, water, poppy seeds, salt, and pepper in a jar with lid; shake well. Pour the dressing over the greens and fruit to bring the salad together. Divide the salad into eight bowls. Place two of the warm grilled chicken tenderloins over the top of each salad. Garnish each salad with about 1 tablespoon Feta cheese. Makes 8 salads.

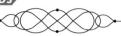

Time: i Hour

AWESOME POTATO SALAD

Note: *This was my mother Ann Fiorino's version of potato salad. It has been handed down to her daughters and granddaughters. I have included it in every cookbook that I write because it is so delicious, especially when served warm. Everyone will want this recipe.*

5 pounds red potatoes

2 teaspoons salt

6 hard-boiled eggs

⅓ cup onion, chopped

⅔ cup tender celery hearts with leaves, chopped small

1 quart Kraft Miracle Whip, or your favorite salad dressing

1 teaspoon yellow mustard

1 teaspoon salt

¼ teaspoon fine ground black pepper

2 slices bacon

2 teaspoons red wine vinegar

1 teaspoon sugar

Paprika

Parsley sprigs

1. Wash and peel potatoes; cut into small quarters, about 1-inch pieces. Boil potatoes in an 8-quart pot in salted water until potatoes are tender but not mushy. Boil eggs until hard-boiled, about 15 minutes. Drain cooked potatoes and place in large mixing bowl. Peel eggs when cooled; chop and add to warm potatoes. Add the onions, celery, salad dressing, mustard, salt, and pepper.

2. Cook the bacon until crisp; remove from heat. Remove all but 1 tablespoon of the bacon drippings. Crunch the bacon up into small pieces and add back to the pan. Add the vinegar and sugar and put back on heat for about 30 seconds to form thin syrup. Add the syrup all at once to the potato salad and mix together until well blended. Sprinkle the top with paprika and garnish top of salad with parsley sprigs. Serves 12.

Time: 20 Minutes

ORANGE MARMALADE
FRUIT SALAD

Note: *This salad is a beautiful combination of fruits tossed in frozen orange juice and marmalade.*
It makes a great taste after a heavy Italian meal.

1 cup fresh blueberries

2 cups fresh strawberries, sliced

1 red apple, skin on, and small quartered

1 green apple, skin on,
  and small quartered

1 cup chunk pineapple, drained

1 cup purple seedless grapes

1½ cups frozen sliced peaches

1 cup honeydew melon balls

1 cup cantaloupe melon balls

½ cup kiwi, sliced small

2 medium bananas sliced
  into 1-inch slices

⅓ cup frozen orange juice

1 to 2 tablespoons orange marmalade

Rinse blueberries, strawberries, and apples with cool water and prepare as directed. Place in a large bowl with pineapple, grapes, peaches, melon balls, kiwi, and bananas. Add the orange juice and marmalade and toss together. Place fruit sald into a large pretty pedestal bowl. Garnish with mint sprigs if desired. Makes 12 servings.

Time: 10 Minutes

SEVEN CUP SALAD

Note: *This salad may not be Italian, but it is one of the best holiday salads ever! It goes well with Italian cuisine.*

1 cup chunk pineapple, drained

1 cup mandarin oranges, drained

1 cup sweet shredded coconut

1 cup sour cream

1 cup pecans, left whole

1 cup miniature marshmallows

1 cup maraschino cherries, drained well

Combine all ingredients in a medium bowl and toss together until well combined. Serve in individual dessert cups or a pretty glass bowl for presentation. Store in refrigerator until ready to serve. Serves 8.

VEGETABLES & SIDE DISHES

When I think about vegetables, I think about the basics of Italian food. We Italians love our vegetables, and they are included in almost every dish we make. They accompany our meat, chicken, and fish entrees and are cooked up along with our pasta dishes. Many of these dishes can even stand alone as complete meals. Thinking about the grand dish of Eggplant Rollatini that features ricotta filled eggplant, smothered in marinara sauce, all I need is a chunk of Italian bread and this meal is complete. Others are so delicious chopped and breaded, like the Italian Breaded Cauliflower, or the Parmesan Crusted Zucchini.

I encourage you to try all of these vegetable dishes, and you may find the things you thought you didn't like becoming one of your favorites. This has been the case with Garlic Crusted Brussels Sprouts and especially the Italian Fried Cabbage, which could be my family's favorite. I even included the dandelion dish that my mother would make every spring: Sicilian Dandelion Greens. She, like so many Sicilian women, would scour the neighborhood looking for these little greens. I personally thought they were a lot of work, rinsing and rinsing them again to get them clean. But yet in her honor, if you want a childhood memory, please indulge yourself. Now let me give you a few tips for the perfect vegetable dishes.

1. If possible, choose fresh vegetables for the best taste.

2. Do not overcook vegetables, they are best cooked to crisp-tender

3. Salting the vegetables while frying them causes them to release moisture, bringing out the flavor.

4. Fry or roast vegetables in extra virgin olive oil and fresh cut garlic for the best flavor.

Time: 15 Minutes

ITALIAN STIR-FRY VEGETABLES

Note: *Stir- fry vegetables are good any time of the year, and usually go with any entrée of meat or fish. This recipe is light and delicious.*

⅓ cup extra virgin olive oil

2 cups broccoli florets

2 cups cauliflower florets

1 bunch fresh asparagus,
   hard ends trimmed and cut into thirds

1 medium zucchini,
   sliced into 2-inch cubes

1 large red bell pepper, sliced thin

1 small onion,
   chopped into small quarters

3 cloves garlic, chopped

1 teaspoon salt

½ teaspoon ground black pepper

¼ teaspoon crushed red pepper flakes

½ cup marinara sauce,
   or ½ cup tomato sauce

Place olive oil in large skillet. Add the broccoli, cauliflower, asparagus, zucchini, bell pepper, and onion. Add the garlic and sprinkle the vegetables with salt, pepper, and red pepper flakes. Stir-fry the vegetables on medium high heat, stirring frequently, for about 10 to 12 minutes, or until vegetables are crisp tender and have a good flavor. Add the marinara sauce and any additional seasonings as desired; simmer an additional 5 minutes. Serves 6.

Time: 15 Minutes

ZESTY ITALIAN ZUCCHINI

Note: *Fresh small zucchini right out of the garden are great for this dish. They are tender without so many seeds. A great side dish to accompany meat, chicken or fish.*

3 to 4 small zucchinis, unpeeled and sliced ¼-inch

¼ cup extra virgin olive oil

1 medium onion, peeled and sliced thin

3 cloves garlic, chopped

1 teaspoon salt

½ teaspoon ground black pepper

2 tablespoons freshly squeezed lemon juice, about ½ lemon

Wash zucchini in water and pat dry. Trim the ends and cut into slices. Place the zucchini in large skillet with olive oil, onion and garlic; sauté over medium heat for about 10 to 12 minutes. Salt and pepper while frying. At the end of cooking, squeeze lemon juice over zucchini and put lid on pan. Let steam for about 1 minute. Remove to platter and serve warm. Serves 4.

Naomi, Alex, and Gia

Time: 1 Hour

STUFFED ZUCCHINI
WITH COUSCOUS

Note: *This could be one of my favorite zucchini dishes. It can be served whole for a main meal course,
or cut in fourths for a side dish. A great summer treat!*

2 medium zucchinis

Olive oil

3 tablespoons olive oil, divided

1 small zucchini, cut into 1-inch pieces

1 small onion, chopped small

2 cloves garlic, chopped fine

2½ cups Kitchen Basics Chicken Stock

½ cup couscous

12 cherry tomatoes

8 fresh basil leaves, chopped coarse

1 teaspoon toasted pine nuts,
   or toasted chopped walnuts

1 teaspoon salt

¼ teaspoon ground black pepper

Crushed red pepper flakes

Cherry tomatoes

Basil sprig

Grated Parmesan cheese

1. Preheat oven to 375 degrees. Gently scrub zucchinis under cool water; pat dry. Remove ends and cut zucchinis in half lengthwise. Place halves top-side down on lightly oiled baking sheet and bake until soft, 10 to 12 minutes. Remove and cool.

2. Scoop out centers of the zucchini leaving a ¼-inch thickness in the shells. Place scooped-out zucchini in a large fry pan with 2 tablespoons olive oil. Wash and gently scrub the small zucchini; remove ends. Add the small chopped zucchini, onion, and garlic to the skillet. Sauté together until lightly browned, 5 to 6 minutes. Add the chicken stock, couscous, and remaining tablespoon olive oil. Bring to boil and cook together about 3 minutes. Add tomatoes, basil leaves, pine nuts, salt, and pepper; toss together.

3. Fill each zucchini shell with couscous mixture and place in a 13x9-inch baking dish, lightly coated with olive oil. Cover with foil and bake in oven for 15 to 20 minutes until set. Remove from oven and garnish with crushed red pepper flakes, cherry tomatoes, and freshly grated Parmesan cheese. Serve whole, or in portions for side servings. Garnish with basil sprigs Serves 2 to 8.

Time: 30 Minutes

PARMESAN CRUSTED ZUCCHINI STICKS

Note: *These zucchini sticks are so delicious, it will be hard to eat just one.*
They are great alone, or dipped in your favorite marinara sauce.

2 medium zucchini

Lawry's coarse garlic salt
with parsley added

3 eggs

1 cup Progresso Style Italian
bread crumbs

⅔ cup Parmesan cheese

2 large cloves garlic, chopped fine

½ teaspoon salt

½ teaspoon pepper

⅛ teaspoon crushed red pepper flakes

Olive oil

Parmesan cheese, optional

1. Preheat oven to 400 degrees. Wash and trim ends of zucchini. Cut the zucchini in half crosswise. Cut each half into 3 wedges, giving 6 wedges per half zucchini. Pierce each wedge several times with fork, careful not to break the wedges. Sprinkle the wedges with the coarse garlic salt; set aside.

2. Beat the eggs and place in a shallow pie plate. Prepare the coating mixture by placing the bread crumbs, cheese, garlic, salt, pepper, and crushed red pepper flakes in another shallow plate. Dip the wedges into the egg and then into the bread crumb coating. Re-dip the coated wedges into the egg a second time and re-coat the wedges. Place the wedges on a lightly oiled cookie sheet, or on parchment paper. With wedges on cookie sheet, lightly drizzle olive oil over the wedges. Bake in hot oven for 20 minutes, or until golden. Remove from oven and sprinkle with Parmesan cheese if desired. Serve while warm. Makes 24 wedges.

Time: 30 Minutes

ITALIAN BREADED CAULIFLOWER

Note: *These breaded cauliflower florets are wonderful as an appetizer, but can also be used as a vegetable side dish.*
If you need more bread crumbs, just make up another batch.

1 large head cauliflower

2 teaspoons salt

3 eggs, beaten

1 cup Progresso Italian Style
  bread crumbs

⅓ cup grated Parmesan cheese

2 cloves garlic, chopped fine

2 tablespoons fresh curly parsley,
  chopped

1 teaspoon salt

¼ teaspoon ground black pepper

Olive oil

Salt and pepper

Parmesan cheese

1. Remove stems from cauliflower, and break cauliflower into small florets. Boil cauliflower
    florets in boiling salted water just until tender, 6 to 8 minutes. Drain and set aside. Beat
    eggs in large bowl and add the florets, mixing gently to coat.

2. Mix the bread crumbs, cheese, garlic, parsley, salt, and pepper together. Place in large
    shallow bowl. With slotted spoon, lift a few of the florets out of the egg mixture and into
    the bread crumbs. Roll in crumbs until well coated. Place coated florets on wax paper on
    cookie sheet until all have been coated with crumbs.

3. Pour olive oil in large skillet or in an electric fry pan, and fry the florets until golden
    brown. Sprinkle salt and pepper over florets while frying. Transfer florets to a paper
    towel, then to a large platter. Continue frying all the florets. If oil in skillet becomes too
    dark, clean pan with paper towel and add new olive oil to continue frying.

4. Sprinkle cheese over the warm cauliflower florets and serve immediately. Serves 6.

Time: 15 Minutes

GOLDEN CRUSTED CAULIFLOWER

Note: *This dish is one of the most popular of Italian sides. Everyone loves this recipe because it is so simple and delicious, and your guests will be raving about it all the way home.*

1 large head cauliflower

⅓ cup extra virgin olive oil

3 cloves garlic, chopped

1 to 2 teaspoons salt

½ teaspoon coarse black pepper

Parmesan cheese

Wash cauliflower and remove hard core and stems up to where florets begin. Break pods into small florets, cutting some in half if still too large. Pour olive oil into large skillet and sauté the garlic and florets together. Continue to stir-fry the cauliflower over medium heat 10 to 12 minutes, adding more olive oil if pan gets dry. The cauliflower should begin to get golden and crusty. Sprinkle with salt and pepper, and cover with lid for 2 to 3 minutes for a crisp tender taste. Cauliflower should be golden, crusty and tender, but not mushy. Remove onto platter, and sprinkle with Parmesan cheese. Serves 6.

Time: 15 Minutes

ITALIAN BREADED EGGPLANT

Note: *I can assure that every Sicilian kid grew up with these wonderful warm and crisp eggplant. We would eat them right off the plate, almost before they got to the table. Short on time? Skip the soaking, they will still be delicious.*

Rosalie's Marinara Sauce,
  recipe on page 160

1 large eggplant

3 teaspoons salt

3 eggs, beaten

2 cups Progresso Italian Style
  bread crumbs

⅔ cup Parmesan cheese

¼ cup fresh curly parsley

3 cloves garlic, chopped fine

½ teaspoon salt

½ teaspoon pepper

Olive oil

Salt

Parmesan Cheese

1. Slice eggplant thin, about ¼-inch thick. Let the eggplant soak in cool salted water for about 20 to 30 minutes. Rinse eggplant, drain and pat dry.

2. Place the eggs in a shallow plate; set aside. Combine the bread crumbs, cheese, parsley, garlic, salt, and pepper in a shallow plate; mix well. Dip the eggplant slices in the beaten eggs and then in bread crumbs, coating well.

3. In large skillet, heat olive oil to medium heat. Fry the eggplant slices in the oil about 2 to 3 minutes on each side. Lightly salt the slices while frying. The slices should be fork tender and crisp. Add more oil as needed for frying. If crumbs begin to burn in bottom of pan before completing the eggplant, clean pan and start a new batch. Drain fried eggplant on paper towels and transfer to platter. Sprinkle with Parmesan cheese and serve, or add marinara sauce for dipping. Makes about 12 to 15 slices, depending on the size of eggplant.

ITALIAN ROASTED VEGETABLES

Note: *These vegetables are delicious roasted in the oven, or can even be put on a skewer and placed on the grill in the summer.*

1 large each red, green, and yellow bell peppers, seeds removed and cut into 2-inch strips

1 small green and yellow zucchini, ends trimmed, and cut into 2-inch slices

2 large onions, peeled and quartered

12 large white button mushrooms, rinsed and left whole

1 pound asparagus, hard ends trimmed, and cut into thirds

4 to 5 small new potatoes, halved

3 cloves garlic, chopped

½ cup fresh basil leaves,
   or 1 teaspoon dried basil

⅔ cup extra virgin olive oil

1 to 2 teaspoons coarse sea salt

1 teaspoon coarse black pepper

1 teaspoon crushed red pepper flakes

1 cup grape tomatoes

2 tablespoons balsamic vinegar

Parmesan cheese, optional

1. Preheat oven to 450 degrees. Place the peppers, zucchini, onion, mushrooms, aspara-gus, and potatoes in very large bowl. Combine the garlic, basil, olive oil, salt, pepper, and red pepper flakes in a jar with lid. Shake well to combine and pour over the vegeta-bles; toss to coat. Place vegetables in a large roasting pan and place in hot oven. Roast uncovered for 25 to 30 minutes, turning once or twice for even roasting.

2. Add the grape tomatoes about 5 minutes before removing from oven and stir into vegetables. Remove from oven and sprinkle vegetables with the balsamic vinegar; add more seasonings and olive oil if desired. Transfer vegetables to a large platter; sprinkle with Parmesan cheese if desired. Serves 8 to 10.

Time: 1 Hour

EGGPLANT ROLLATINI

Note: *I can't decide how delicious these are, you may just have to experience them for yourself. Purchase a small meat slicer or a mandolin in kitchen specialty shops to slice the eggplant thin.*

1 recipe **Rosalie's Marinara Sauce**
  on page 160

1 large eggplant, about 4-inch diameter

4 cups cool water

1 tablespoon salt

1 cup Progresso Italian Style
  bread crumbs

⅔ cup grated Parmesan cheese

3 cloves garlic, chopped fine

¼ cup fresh curly parsley, chopped

3 eggs

Salt and pepper

1 (15-ounce) carton ricotta cheese

1 cup shredded mozzarella cheese

½ cup Pecorino Romano
  or Parmesan cheese

¼ cup fresh curly parsley, chopped

1 egg

⅛ teaspoon black ground pepper

⅓ cup olive oil

½ cup grated Parmesan cheese

1. Preheat oven to 375 degrees. Prepare the marinara according to directions; set aside. Cut stem and end from eggplant. Peel the eggplant partially in strips, leaving some of the peel intact. Using a meat cutter or a mandolin, slice the eggplant into lengthwise slices, about ⅛" thick. Let the eggplant slices soak in cool water with salt added for about 20 minutes while you prepare breading and filling.

2. Combine the breading by placing the bread crumbs, cheese, garlic, and parsley in a shallow pie plate; toss well and set aside. Beat eggs and place in another shallow pie plate; set aside.

3. Prepare the filling by placing the ricotta, mozzarella, Pecorino Romano, parsley, egg, and pepper in a bowl. Mix well and set aside.

4. Rinse the eggplant in cool water and drain. Dip each slice in the beaten egg and then in the bread crumb mixture on both sides. Place the olive oil in a large skillet and over medium heat, fry the eggplant about 2 minutes on each side until golden. Salt and pepper lightly as they fry. Drain slices on paper towels. Add olive oil to pan as needed, and if necessary, start a clean pan midway through frying. When all of the eggplant slices have been drained, place them on a large cookie sheet. Place 2 tablespoons ricotta filling on each slice, and spread gently. Starting from the short end of the slice, roll the eggplant up jelly-roll style. Place each roll seam-side down and leave on baking sheet.

5. Spray a 13x9-inch baking pan with cooking spray. Pour 1 cup of the marinara in bottom of baking pan. Place each roll seam-side down in the baking pan. There should be about 15 rolls. If all rolls do not fit, use an additional smaller pan. Pour marinara sauce over the rolls, about 2 cups. Top with Parmesan cheese. Cover loosely with aluminum foil. Bake about 25 minutes, until bubbly on sides. Serves 8.

Time: 20 Minutes

BRAISED SWISS CHARD

Note: *I can remember eating this dish as a child. My mother always had a big pot of greens on the stove and this was one of my favorites.*

1 pound Swiss chard, stems removed

¼ cup extra virgin olive oil

2 cloves garlic, chopped

½ teaspoon salt

¼ teaspoon black ground pepper

⅔ cup fresh tomatoes, chopped,
   or ⅔ cup diced tomatoes with juice

¼ teaspoon sugar

1 cup water

Salt and pepper

1. Wash and rinse the Swiss chard three times in cold water to remove any dirt or sand. Trim ends and cut the long stalks in fourths. Place the olive oil in a large skillet and sauté the garlic for about 30 seconds, stirring constantly until light golden. Add the Swiss chard, salt, and pepper.

2. Add the tomatoes and sprinkle the sugar over the tomatoes. Add the water and steam the Swiss chard with the lid on for about 15 minutes, or until the chard is tender and the flavors are combined. Taste, and add any additional seasonings. Serves 4.

Time: 25 Minutes

SICILIAN DANDELION GREENS

Note: *Every spring, my mother, Ann Fiorino, would scour our neighborhood gathering dandelions. She would go out with her little knife and bag, and with great joy pick up the greens. If you do this, stick to plants that are not blooming for a less bitter taste. She would rinse and rinse in a large bowl, until the water at the bottom was free of dirt. She would then either boil them or fry them in a large fry pan. This recipe is in honor of her*

1 large bunch dandelion greens, picked fresh,
   or market garden grown

1 teaspoon salt

¼ cup extra virgin olive oil

1 teaspoon salt

3 cloves garlic, chopped

Coarse black pepper

¼ teaspoon crushed red pepper flakes, optional

1. Wash and rinse the dandelion greens several times until there is no longer dirt in the bottom of the bowl. In 3-quart pot boiling salted water, par-boil the dandelions for 4 to 5 minutes. Drain the dandelions and save liquid if desired. (Liquid from cooked greens is very medicinal.)

2. In large skillet, pour in the olive oil. Add the drained greens, salt, garlic, pepper, and crushed red pepper flakes. Place lid over greens, and continue to steam dandelions until they are as soft as you like. Taste the greens and if too bitter, add a little more salt and olive oil. Serve with hard Italian bread. Servings not determined.

Time: 1 Hour

ITALIAN FRIED CABBAGE

Note: *This is a favorite dish that my husband and children love. Tender slices of fried cabbage topped with a delicious marinara sauce makes this dish irresistible, even if you don't like cabbage.*

1 recipe **Rosalie's Marinara Sauce** found on page 160

1 medium head cabbage

3 quarts water

2 teaspoons salt

1 cup flour

¼ cup grated Parmesan cheese

1 teaspoon Lawry's coarse garlic salt
  with parsley added

¼ teaspoon ground black pepper

3 eggs

1 cup olive oil, divided

1 cup freshly grated Parmesan cheese, divided

Freshly ground coarse black pepper

1. Wash cabbage and remove outer leaves. Place on cutting board and cut the cabbage in half, and then in halves again. Boil cabbage quarters in salted water until tender, about 15 minutes. Drain cabbage and place on cutting board. Let cabbage cool slightly and cut the quarters into ½-inch slices, trying to keep the slices together.

2. In shallow plate, place flour, cheese, garlic salt, and pepper; mix well. Place eggs in another shallow plate and beat until fluffy; set aside. Prepare large skillet with half of the olive oil; place on medium heat.

3. Gently lay the cabbage slices in the egg mixture and lift with slotted spatula to drain. Place egg-coated cabbage slices into the seasoned flour, turning to coat both sides. Fry the cabbage in medium hot oil 2 to 3 minutes on each side until golden crusted. Remove slices to baking pan. Continue to fry until all slices and pieces of cabbage are used, adding remaining olive oil as you go along.

4. Arrange some of the slices in a single layer on a large platter. Cover with part of the marinara sauce and sprinkle with cheese. Continue to layer the cabbage, using marinara and cheese. Garnish last layer with remaining cheese and freshly ground coarse black pepper. Serves 6.

Time: 20 Minutes

ITALIAN FRIED PEPPERS

Note: *My mother would often make this wonderful dish and serve it with garlic grilled chicken or with Italian sausage.*

1 large red bell pepper

1 large yellow bell pepper

1 large green bell pepper

⅓ cup extra virgin olive oil

2 cloves garlic, chopped

Salt and pepper

½ teaspoon crushed red pepper flakes

1 (8-ounce) can tomato sauce

¼ cup water

½ teaspoon sugar

½ teaspoon balsamic vinegar

Grated Parmesan cheese, optional

1. Wash, core, and remove seeds from peppers; cut into julienne pieces, not too thin. Place peppers in large skillet with olive oil and garlic, and stir-fry 10 to 12 minutes over medium heat. Peppers should be crisp, not mushy. Salt and pepper the peppers while they fry and add the crushed red pepper flakes.

2. Add the tomato sauce, water and sugar. Cook together on low heat about 5 more minutes. Add the balsamic vinegar and stir. Taste, and add more seasoning if desired. Transfer to serving bowl, and garnish with Parmesan cheese if desired. Serves 4 to 6.

Time: 30 Minutes

GARLIC CRUSTED
BRUSSELS SPROUTS

Note: *People who don't like Brussels sprouts love these because they are infused with the good olive oil and crusted on the outside with garlic. The smaller the better is a good rule for tenderness*

1 pound small fresh Brussels sprouts

2 quarts water

1 teaspoon salt

⅓ cup extra virgin olive oil

3 cloves garlic, chopped fine

½ to 1 teaspoon salt

¼ teaspoon ground black pepper

1. Wash and drain Brussels sprouts. Place in a 3-quart pot with 2 quarts water and salt. Bring to boil and cook sprouts for 20 minutes, or until tender; drain well. Frozen Brussels sprouts can also be used, and boiled in the same way.

2. Place olive oil in skillet with garlic, and heat for about 30 seconds, careful not to burn. Add the drained Brussels sprouts and the salt and pepper. Stir the sprouts often until they become crusted with the oil and garlic, about 6 to 8 minutes. Cut a few of them in half while they are still frying. Transfer to serving bowl and serve warm. Serves 4 to 6.

Time: 50 Minutes

ITALIAN ROASTED POTATOES

Note: *These roasted potatoes are golden crunchy and coated with chopped garlic and herbs. This is a great dish for most any entrée.*

2 to 3 large russet potatoes cubed small, about 5 cups

⅓ cup extra virgin olive oil

4 cloves garlic, chopped fine

1 teaspoon dried basil

1 teaspoon dried oregano

½ teaspoon red pepper flakes

1 teaspoon coarse sea salt

½ teaspoon coarse black pepper

1. Preheat oven to 400 degrees. Place potatoes in a medium bowl; set aside.

2. Place olive oil, garlic, basil, oregano, red pepper flakes, salt, and pepper in a jar with lid. Shake the jar well to mix the oil and herbs. Pour the olive oil mixture over the potatoes and toss to coat. Spread the potatoes onto ungreased cookie sheet. Bake uncovered for 35 to 40 minutes, or until golden brown and tender. Stir potatoes during baking once or twice to brown evenly. Drizzle with additional olive oil if potatoes become too dry. Remove to serving dish, or spoon around roasted meat on platter. Serves 6 to 8.

Ross David & Taylor

Time:30 Minutes

GARLIC CHEESE MASHED POTATOES WITH CHIVES

Note: *I can't remember having this dish growing up in an Italian family, but it has taken on a very popular liking and I wanted to add it to the menu. Mince the garlic with a chopper, or use a garlic press. The Yukon gold potatoes are buttery and just right for this dish. This recipe is absolutely delicious!*

10 medium Yukon gold potatoes, about 3 pounds

3 quarts water

2 teaspoons salt

¾ cup half-and-half

½ cup butter

½ cup sour cream

½ teaspoon salt

⅛ teaspoon ground black pepper

2 gloves garlic, minced

1 cup shredded mozzarella cheese

Fresh chives

1. Wash and peel potatoes and cut in quarters. Boil potatoes in a 3-quart heavy pot in salted water for 20 minutes, or until tender. Drain well and keep in strainer.

2. In same pot, combine half-and-half and butter; heat together until butter is melted. Add the potatoes back into the butter mixture and using a hand held masher, mash potatoes until smooth.

3. Add the sour cream, salt, pepper, garlic, and cheese; stir with slotted spoon until potatoes are smooth and flavored. Spoon potatoes into large bowl and garnish top with fresh snipped chives. Serves 8 to 10.

Sebastian Schultz

Time: 10 Minutes

SAUTÉED SPINACH WITH GARLIC

Note: *This wonderful side dish of spinach is so delicious and quick to make, you will have it often. Even the children love this one.*

¼ cup extra virgin olive oil

3 cloves garlic, chopped

1 (10-ounce) bag fresh baby spinach

½ teaspoon coarse sea salt

¼ teaspoon coarse ground black pepper

Parmesan cheese, optional

In large skillet, sauté the garlic in the olive oil until barely golden, about 30 seconds. Place the spinach over the olive oil and garlic and add the salt and pepper. Heat together about 2 to 3 minutes, stirring often until the spinach is wilted but still firm. Taste and add more seasonings if desired. Remove to platter and sprinkle with Parmesan cheese if desired. Serve while warm. Serves 4.

Time: 15 Minutes

ITALIAN FRIED ASPARAGUS

Note: *There is nothing like fresh-cut asparagus sautéed in garlic with butter and olive oil. Yum!*

1 pound fresh young asparagus, ends trimmed

2 cloves garlic, finely chopped

2 to 3 tablespoons extra virgin olive oil

1 tablespoon butter

Coarse sea salt

Coarse ground black pepper

Wash and rinse asparagus and trim off tough ends. Leave asparagus whole. In large skillet, place the asparagus, garlic, and olive oil. Sauté the asparagus over medium heat for 8 to 10 minutes, stirring often. Add the butter and place lid over asparagus to steam crisp tender. Add salt and pepper to taste. Serve warm. Serves 4.

Time: 20 Minutes

Green Beans with Garlic Crusted Potatoes

Note: *These green beans are perfect with most any entrée, and have an addicting flavor.*

2 to 3 medium red potatoes, skins left on

⅓ cup extra virgin olive oil

1 teaspoon Lawry's garlic salt with parsley added

2 cloves garlic, chopped fine

1 pound fresh or frozen green beans

Salt and pepper to taste

¼ cup water, if needed

1. Wash potatoes and cut into small chunks. Place potatoes in large fry pan with olive oil. Sprinkle potatoes with garlic salt. Add the chopped garlic. If using the fresh green beans, add them now and let them cook with potatoes until crisp tender, about 10 to 12 minutes, adding water if needed. Salt and pepper as desired.

2. If using frozen green beans, sauté the potatoes in the oil for about 6 to 7 minutes until almost tender. Add the fresh frozen green beans at this time. Season with salt and pepper as desired. Complete frying the green beans with the potatoes until green beans are crisp tender. Remove to serving dish and serve warm. Serves 4.

BREADS, ROLLS & PIZZA

Let's Bake Bread

Bread is, and always has been, a necessity of life. The baking of bread goes all the way back to Bible days and to the ancient days of Rome. By far it is the most sought after staple in every culture and cuisine. I think we can all agree that there just nothing more sensual than a kitchen filled with the aroma of baking bread. Most all of us have memories of our mothers or grandmothers baking our favorite rolls, biscuits, breads, and even homemade pizzas. It is the one thing that will draw us into the kitchen, and cause us to beg the cook for just one little taste.

Bread to Italians is like bees to honey. We love to lather it with olive oil, herbs, garlic, and cheese. We use it fresh right out of the oven, and when it gets hard, we use it in our soups, salads, and for the best sliced toast in the world. You will love the Homemade Italian Bread, the Italian Sausage Pizza, or even the wonderful Homemade Garlic Breadsticks among the recipes in this section.

The following tips are things I learned from my mother, and from just practicing:

1. Use a good grade of flour like Gold Medal or Pillsbury.

2. Get a good fast-rise yeast such as Fleischmann's.

3. Don't leave out the salt, and don't be afraid to use the amount listed in the recipe.

4. Make sure the water is lukewarm: 110 degrees. Let the yeast and water dissolve together until the yeast foams up, about 8 minutes.

5. Use pizza stones for the best crust, and place stones in the middle of the oven for best surrounding heat.

6. Use cornmeal sprinkled on the pizza stone before placing bread on stone.

7. Pre-heat oven to at least 400 degrees, and let the bread come to a golden brown, about 30 minutes of baking time.

Bruschetta Bread
on page 118

Time: 4 Hours

ROSALIE'S HOMEMADE ITALIAN BREAD

Note: *This is the Italian bread that I grew up with as a child. We would eat it right out of the oven slathered with olive oil and Parmesan cheese. Oh, what a treat!*

1 (14-inch) pizza stone

2 tablespoons yellow cornmeal

6½ to 7 cups all-purpose flour

3 teaspoons salt

2 tablespoons active dry yeast

2 cups warm water, about 110 degrees

1 tablespoon olive oil

1 egg, beaten

1 tablespoon water

Sesame seeds

1. Preheat oven to 400 degrees. Place the 6½ cups flour and salt into a large bowl; mix together. Put yeast in warm water and stir to dissolve; let the yeast foam up for 6 to 8 minutes. Make a well in the flour and add a little of the yeast water with a small amount of flour; bring the flour together and set to side of bowl. Continue to add a little water and flour until all the water has been used. Bring all the dough together; dough may be sticky. Work in the remaining ½ cup flour as needed. If dough comes together firm, you will not need the additional flour. Knead the bread for 8 to 10 minutes or until the dough feels elastic. Keep the dough in the same bowl and pour the olive oil over the top; turn the dough to coat the other side. Place a thin towel over the dough and place the bowl in a warm place. Let rise for 1½ to 2 hours, or until doubled in size.

2. Punch the dough down, and let rise for another hour. If pressed for time, bypass this step.

3. After the second rising, punch the dough down and divide the dough into three parts. Sprinkle cornmeal onto the stone; set aside. Shape each part of dough into an oblong loaf and place on the stone; place each loaf 2 inches apart. Using a serrated knife, make 3 slits across the top of each loaf. Beat the egg and water together and brush each loaf with the egg wash; sprinkle with sesame seeds. Place a warm loose towel over the top of loaves and let rise until double in size, about 1 hour.

4. Place the stone on middle grate in oven and bake bread for 30 to 35 minutes. The bread should have a golden hard crust. Remove bread from oven and let cool 5 to 10 minutes before slicing. Serve warm with butter or olive oil. Yields 3 loaves.

Time: 10 Minutes

OLIVE OIL HERB DIP

Note: *This dipping oil was served at our table at the famous Carrabba's restaurant in Naples, Florida.
The flavor was intense and wonderfully delicious. It took me a few tries to replicate it, and I hope you enjoy it as much as I did.
Pack the teaspoons full when measuring the herbs.*

1 teaspoon fresh oregano, chopped

1 teaspoon fresh basil, chopped

1 teaspoon fresh flat-leaf parsley, chopped

1 teaspoon fresh rosemary leaves, chopped

2 cloves garlic, minced

Pinch of granulated garlic

¼ teaspoon crushed red pepper flakes

2 tablespoons extra virgin olive oil

⅛ teaspoon coarse sea salt

⅛ teaspoon coarse ground black pepper

Crusty Italian bread

Olive oil for bread plates

Place the oregano, basil, parsley, and rosemary in a wooden bowl. Add the garlic and using a pestle, pound the herbs and garlic together. Add the granulated garlic, red pepper flakes, olive oil, salt, and pepper. Stir the herbs and olive oil mixture together. To serve, place 1 to 2 table-spoons olive oil on bread plate and add ½ teaspoon herb mixture. Dip crusty Italian bread into the oil. Makes ten ½ teaspoon servings.

Time: 3 Hours and 45 Minutes

SESAME SEED DINNER ROLLS

Note: *These rolls are crusty on the outside and dense on the inside. They are absolutely delicious!*

1 (14-inch) pizza stone

2 tablespoons yellow cornmeal

1¼ cup warm water

3 teaspoons yeast

4½ cups all-purpose flour

2 teaspoons salt

1 egg, beaten

2 tablespoons butter, melted

2 teaspoons olive oil

1 egg white

1 tablespoon water

Sesame seeds

1. Preheat oven to 400 degrees. Put yeast in warm water and stir to dissolve; let the yeast foam up for 8 minutes. Place the flour in a large bowl; add the salt and mix well. Make a well in the center of the flour and add the egg and melted butter. Add the yeast water a little at a time with the flour. Work the liquid into the flour until all incorporated. Bring the dough together into a ball and knead 8 to 10 minutes, until dough feels elastic. If the dough is sticky, add a little more flour. Pour the olive oil over the dough and turn to coat. Let rise in a warm place for 1½ to 2 hours, or until doubled in size.

2. Punch the dough down and let it rest for 15 minutes. Divide the dough into 12 pieces and shape into rolls. Sprinkle the stone with cornmeal and place the rolls on the stone. Cover rolls and let rise another 1 hour.

3. Beat the egg white with water until foamy. Brush the rolls with the egg white and sprinkle with sesame seeds. Bake in hot oven 20 minutes or until golden. Makes 12 large rolls.

Time: 3 Hours and 30 Minutes

OLIVE ROSEMARY BREAD

Note: *This bread has the wonderful aroma of rosemary, and has a golden crispy crust.
The Kalamata olives have a distinct flavor, and make this bread unique and delicious.*

1 (14-inch) pizza stone

2 tablespoons yellow cornmeal

1 tablespoon active dry yeast

2 teaspoons extra virgin olive oil

1½ cups warm water

1 cup Kalamata olives, pitted and
    chopped

2 tablespoons fresh rosemary, finely
    chopped or 1 tablespoon dried
    rosemary

5 cups all-purpose flour

3 teaspoons salt

2 teaspoons olive oil

1. Preheat oven to 400 degrees. Put yeast and olive oil in warm water. Stir to dissolve, letting it foam up for 8 minutes. Drain olives and add the rosemary to the olives; set aside.

2. In a large bowl, combine the flour and salt; mix together well. Add the olive-rosemary mixture and stir into the flour. Make a well in the center of the flour and add the yeast water a little at a time, gathering flour into it and setting to side of bowl. Continue until all the flour and water have been brought together. Gather the dough into a ball and knead 8 to 10 minutes, until dough feels elastic. Pour olive oil over bread to coat and let rise 1½ to 2 hours, or until doubled in size.

3. Punch dough down and on floured board, cut dough into 2 parts. Let dough rest for 15 minutes. Sprinkle stone with cornmeal and shape dough into 2 loaves. Place loaves on stone and let rise another 1 hour.

4. Make 2 cuts across the top of loaves with serrated knife. Bake for 28 to 30 minutes, until bread is golden on top. Makes 2 loaves.

BRAIDED EASTER BREAD

Note: *I did not grow up with Easter Bread, but always wanted to make it. This beautiful braided bread is perfect for the Easter Centerpiece. Complete with dyed Easter eggs, this sweet bread is perfect.*

1 (14-inch) pizza stone

1 tablespoon cornmeal

1½ cups hot milk

½ cup sugar

1 tablespoon salt

½ cup salted butter

2 tablespoons yeast

½ cup warm water, 110 degrees

6½ cups all-purpose flour, divided

2 eggs beaten

2 teaspoons olive oil

2 tablespoons butter, melted

2 tablespoons sesame seeds

5 hard-boiled eggs, dyed in same color or varied

¾ cup powdered sugar

1 to 2 tablespoons milk

½ teaspoon almond extract

Colored sprinkles

1. Preheat oven to 375 degrees. Place milk in small saucepan and bring milk to hot tempera-ture, but not to boiling. Add the sugar, salt, and butter. Stir milk until butter melts and sugar is dissolved. Remove from heat and cool to lukewarm.

2.   Place the yeast in the warm water, and let stand until foamy, about 8 minutes. Stir the yeast mixture into the lukewarm milk mixture. (Make sure the milk is not too warm to kill the yeast.)

3.   Place 3 cups flour in a large bowl. Make a well in the flour and add the beaten eggs. Add the milk and yeast mixture to the eggs. Using a fork, beat the flour, eggs, and milk mixture for 2 to 3 minutes. Add the remainder 3½ cups flour and mix with clean hands until dough is stiff enough to leave side of bowl. Dough will be sticky; flour hands to handle dough. Knead the dough for 2 to 3 minutes until smooth and elastic. Pour olive oil over dough, and turn to coat. Cover with thin towel and place in warm place, free of drafts. Let the dough rise for 1½ hours, or until doubled in size.

4.   Punch the dough down, and place the dough on a floured counter. Divide the dough into three sections. Using floured hands, roll each dough section into a 24-inch long rope. Lay the three dough ropes side by side and starting from the bottom, braid the ropes together. Form the braided bread into a round ring, pinching the ends together. Place the ring on the pizza stone, sprinkled with cornmeal. Brush melted butter over the ring. Sprinkle the ring with sesame seeds. Place towel over bread ring, and let rise for 1 hour. When bread has risen, tuck the dyed eggs in between the braids around the ring. Be sure the dyed eggs have completely dried to prevent food coloring from running. Place the stone with the bread ring in the center of the oven for even browning. Bake for 40 to 45 minutes, or until golden brown.

5.   Remove the bread ring and let cool on counter. Place powdered sugar in small bowl. Add the milk and almond extract to make a thin glaze. Drizzle the glaze over the bread and sprinkle with colored sprinkles. Gently remove the braided ring from the pizza stone onto a pretty round tray, keeping the eggs intact. Place tray in center of table if desired for centerpiece. Serves 10 to 12.

Time: 1 Hour and 15 Minutes

IRISH SODA BREAD

Note: *Oops! Irish Soda Bread? Well, this recipe is so good and delicious, I thought you might want to serve it to your Irish friends around St. Patrick's Day. It is a sweet bread with a delicious texture and a crunchy crust that makes it mouth-watering good!*

1 (14-inch) pizza stone

1 tablespoon cornmeal

5½ cups all-purpose flour

¾ cup sugar

2 teaspoons baking powder

1 teaspoon baking soda

1½ teaspoons salt

½ cup sweet cream butter

¾ cup mixed light and dark raisins

2 tablespoons caraway seeds

1 egg

2 cups buttermilk

1. Preheat oven to 350 degrees. Place flour, sugar, baking powder, baking soda, and salt in a large sifter. Sift the ingredients together until the flour is light and mixed well. Cut the butter into the flour and mix the butter and flour with your hands until it gets grainy. Stir in the raisins and caraway seeds.

2. Add the egg and buttermilk in a bowl and beat together until well blended. Make a well in the middle of the flour and add the buttermilk mixture; stir together until the dough comes together. Flour hands in order to handle the dough; dough will be sticky. Place about 1 tablespoon cornmeal onto the pizza stone. Divide the dough into two round loaves and place loaves on the stone. Let the bread sit on the stone for about 30 minutes; bread will rise. Place bread in oven and bake for 45 to 50 minutes or until the loaves are golden brown. Do not over bake bread. Let the bread rest for about 10 minutes before cutting. Serve warm with butter. Makes two large loaves.

ITALIAN STUFFED SAUSAGE BREAD

Note: *This Italian stuffed bread is bursting with flavor. Much like a large calzone, this bread if filled with spicy sausage, cheeses, and herbs. You will love it! (Shown on page 3).*

1 (14-inch) pizza stone

1 tablespoon cornmeal

3 cups bread flour

1½ teaspoon salt

2 teaspoons active dry yeast

1¼ cup warm water, temperature 110 degrees

2 teaspoons olive oil

1 pound ground Italian sausage, sweet or spicy

1 tablespoon olive oil

1 egg, beaten

½ cup grated Parmesan cheese

1 (8-ounce) package shredded mozzarella cheese

¼ teaspoon oregano

¼ teaspoon crushed red pepper flakes

2 tablespoons fresh curly parsley

Salt and Pepper

1 egg white

1 tablespoon water

Sesame seeds

Grated Parmesan cheese

1. Preheat oven to 350 degrees. Place flour in large bowl; add salt and mix together. Place yeast in warm water and stir to dissolve, letting it foam up for 8 to 10 minutes.

2. Make a well in the flour, and add a little of the yeast water with a small amount of flour, working together and setting the moistened flour to side of bowl. Continue until all the flour and water have been used. Bring all the dough together and knead 8 to 10 minutes until dough feels elastic. Pour olive oil over the dough, turning to coat entire surface. Place towel over dough and let rise in warm place, 1½ to 2 hours, or until doubled in size.

3. Punch dough down and let rest for about 15 minutes. While dough is resting, fry sausage in lightly oiled skillet until browned and crumbled. Remove sausage to medium bowl. Add the egg, cheeses, oregano, red pepper flakes, and parsley. Using a fork, mix the sausage mixture well until it comes together; set aside.

4. Roll dough out on floured counter turning as needed to avoid sticking and adding flour as needed. Roll dough into a 14-inch circle. Spread the meat mixture over the dough to within 1 inch of the edge of the circle. Salt and pepper the meat lightly. Roll the dough jelly-roll style, placing the roll seam-side down on the counter. Shape the roll slightly into a crescent moon shape.

5. Sprinkle cornmeal over the stone and lift the roll from counter and place over the cornmeal. Place the egg white and water into a small bowl. With fork, beat the egg mixture until foamy. Using a brush, spread the egg white over the top of the bread. Sprinkle sesame seeds over the egg white. Bake for 45 minutes. Remove bread and let cool for 10 to 15 minutes. Slice while still warm and drizzle with olive oil. Garnish the bread with grated cheese. Serves 10 to 12.

Rosalie Serving Best Loved Italian

Time: 2 Hours and 30 Minutes

FOCACCIA BREAD WITH MOZZARELLA & TOMATOES

Note: *Focaccia bread is thicker than pizza and very easy to make. Usually made with a liberal amount of oil and herbs, it is baked on stones. Dimple the dough with your fingertips before baking.*

1 (14-inch) pizza stone

1 tablespoon cornmeal

1 tablespoon active dry yeast

¾ cup warm water

3 cups all-purpose flour

1½ teaspoons salt

1 tablespoon olive oil

2 tablespoons olive oil, divided

½ pound fresh mozzarella cheese, drained

3 fresh Roma tomatoes

1 teaspoon herbs de Province

15 fresh basil leaves

Coarse sea salt

Freshly coarse ground black pepper

Freshly grated Parmesan cheese

1. Preheat the oven to 425 degrees. Dissolve the yeast in the water and let stand 8 minutes to foam up. In a large bowl, combine the flour and salt; mix together. Add the yeast water a little at a time, gathering flour into it and setting to side of bowl. Continue until all the flour and water have been brought together. When all flour and water have been used, bring the flour together into a ball. Knead the dough 8 to 10 minutes, until elastic. Pour 1 tablespoon olive oil over dough, turning to coat. Place towel over dough and let rise 1½ hours.

2. Punch dough down and let rest 15 minutes. On floured counter, roll dough to a 12-inch circle. Sprinkle pizza stone with cornmeal. Place circle of dough on stone and brush with 1 tablespoon olive oil. Dimple the dough with your fingertips. Slice the mozzarella ¼-inch thick. Place the sliced mozzarella on dough starting with outer circle and working in. Slice the Roma tomatoes into 12 slices. Place the tomatoes on or near the mozzarella. Sprinkle with herbs de Provence and top with basil leaves.

3. Sprinkle lightly with coarse salt and pepper to taste. Drizzle remaining tablespoon of olive oil over bread. Bake on stone for 20 minutes or until golden. Sprinkle the Parmesan over the warm bread and serve. Serves 8.

Time: 1½ Hours

HOMEMADE GARLIC BREADSTICKS

Note: *Love those breadsticks at the Italian restaurants? Now you can make them yourselves, all hot and buttery and really delicious.*

1 tablespoon active dry yeast

1½ cups warm water, 110 degrees

2 tablespoons sugar

4½ cups all-purpose flour

1 teaspoon salt

¼ cup sweet cream butter, melted

1 tablespoon olive oil

1 to 2 large baking sheets

Parchment paper

Topping

½ cup butter, melted

½ teaspoon kosher salt

¼ teaspoon granulated garlic

⅛ teaspoon dried oregano

½ cup butter, melted

Parmesan cheese

1. Preheat oven to 400 degrees. Put yeast in warm water and add sugar; let stand for about 7 to 8 minutes to allow yeast to activate. Place flour and salt in a large bowl; mix together. Make a well in the flour, and add melted butter and the yeast water. With clean hands, mix the flour and liquid together, until the dough comes together in a ball.

2. Turn the dough out onto floured counter, and knead until smooth and elastic, about 3 to 4 minutes. Place dough in large bowl and pour olive oil over the dough; turning once to coat. Cover with light towel and let rise for 45 minutes, or until doubled in size.

3. Punch dough down and turn onto floured counter. Cut the dough ball in half. Pinch off about 6 to 7 portions from each dough ball. Knead each piece slightly and roll into a 6 to 7-inch breadstick. Twist the breadstick if desired and place on parchment paper on baking sheet, 2 inches apart.

4. Making the topping by placing the melted butter into a small bowl. Add the kosher salt, granulated garlic, and oregano. Brush the breadsticks with the butter topping. Let breadsticks rise uncovered in a warm place for 20 minutes.

5. Place breadsticks in prepared oven and bake for about 15 to 18 minutes. Remove from oven and brush with additional butter. Sprinkle with Parmesan cheese and serve warm. Makes 12 to 14 breadsticks.

Rosalie Serving Best Loved Italian

Time: 15 Minutes

BRUSCHETTA BREAD

Note: *Bruschetta bread is any toasted bread with toppings as few as olive oil, cheese, and garlic.
It is truly your own creation, adding your Italian favorites.*

1 loaf crusty Italian or French bread

3 to 4 tablespoons extra virgin olive oil

3 cloves garlic, minced, divided

1 cup favorite marinara sauce

Pepperoni or Italian sausage, fried and crumbled

½ cup Parmesan cheese

1 cup shredded mozzarella, divided

Crushed red pepper flakes

Fresh basil leaves, optional

1. Preheat oven to 400 degrees. With large serrated knife, slice a long loaf of crusty bread crosswise in half. Brush the cut sides with olive oil and spread the garlic over the olive oil. Place loves in the oven on grate until toasted, about 5 to 6 minutes. Remove loaves to cookie sheet.

2. Spoon marinara sauce over the toasted loaves and add your choice of pepperoni or sausage. Sprinkle Parmesan cheese over the meat toppings, and then add the mozzarella. Sprinkle the loaves with red pepper flakes as much as desired. Place back in the oven for about 5 minutes, or until the cheeses are melted. Garnish loaves with fresh basil leaves. Cut into 4-inch squares. Serves 4 to 8.

Time: 10 Minutes

MODIGA (ITALIAN TOASTED BREAD CRUMBS)

Note: *This is a well-known garnish in the Italian cuisine. Use it over pasta dishes, both red and cream sauces, and over some vegetable and fish dishes.*

1 tablespoon olive oil

1 clove garlic, chopped fine

½ cup plain bread crumbs

Heat olive oil in small pan. Add the garlic and sauté about 15 seconds. Add bread crumbs all at once, stirring constantly until crumbs become darker in color and are "toasted," about 2 minutes. Remove from pan into small bowl. Use about 1 tablespoon of crumbs to garnish individual pasta dishes.

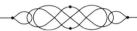

Time: 2 Hours

BASIC PIZZA DOUGH

Note: *This recipe makes two 14-inch pizzas.*

2 (14-inch) pizza stones	4 cups all-purpose flour
Cornmeal	2 teaspoons salt
2 teaspoons active dry yeast	2 teaspoons olive oil
1½ cups warm water, 110 degrees	

1. Preheat oven to 425 degrees. Put yeast in warm water and stir to dissolve, letting the yeast foam up for 8 minutes. Mix the flour and salt together in a large bowl. Add the yeast water a little at a time with small amounts of flour. Set the flour to the side of the bowl. Continue until all the water and flour have been used. Bring the flour together and form dough into a ball. Knead the dough 8 to 10 minutes until soft and elastic. Place dough in large bowl and pour olive oil over dough, turning to coat. Cover with towel and let rise 1½ hours.

2. Punch dough down and let rest on counter for 15 minutes. Cut dough in half, and use each half to make one 14-inch pizza. On floured counter, roll the dough out a little at a time, letting the dough rest before proceeding. Pizza dough can be stretched a little at a time without leaving holes if the dough can rest in intervals.

3. Roll dough to fit pizza stone, about a 14-inch circle. Place cornmeal on stone before placing the dough to avoid sticking. Proceed with toppings and bake for 10 to 15 minutes.

Time: 2½ Hours

WHITE PIZZA WITH
GARLIC CHICKEN & SPINACH

Note: *This pizza is very different from the traditional red sauce and meat combination. Instead, it features basil pesto topped with chicken and lots of cheeses with fresh tomatoes. If pressed for time, ready-made pesto sauce can be used.*

2 (14-inch) pizza stones

2 tablespoons cornmeal, divided

1 recipe **Basic Pizza Dough**,
  found on page 119

1 recipe **Basil Pesto**, found on page 162

2 pounds chicken tenderloins, divided

Lawry's coarse garlic salt with dried
  parsley

Extra virgin olive oil

10 slices provolone cheese
  from deli, divided

1 cup sun dried tomatoes, divided

1 cup button mushrooms,
  sliced thick, divided

4 cups fresh baby spinach, divided

4 cups shredded mozzarella, divided

1 ball fresh buffalo mozzarella, cut thin
  and divided

1 teaspoon red pepper flakes, divided

Fresh large tomato, small quartered
  or 1 cup cherry tomatoes, left whole,
  divided

Extra virgin olive

½ cup grated Parmesan cheese, divided

Fresh Basil leaves, torn, optional

1. Preheat oven to 425 degrees. Prepare pizza dough as instructed for two pizzas. Place the pizza dough on pizza stones, and continue to roll or stretch until the circle is to the edge of the stone. Place cornmeal below the pizza dough. Let dough rise for at least 30 minutes while preparing topping.

2. Prepare the basil pesto as instructed; set aside.

3. Rinse chicken in cool water. Place chicken on cutting board and slice the tenderloins in half. Sprinkle garlic salt on strips and sauté chicken in olive oil until no pink remains, about 3 to 4 minutes; set aside.

4. Brush pizzas with the pesto sauce, covering the pizzas well. Lay five provolone cheese slices over the pesto sauce on each pizza. Lay chicken strips over provolone, about 8 strips to each pizza. Divide the sun-dried tomatoes and mushrooms between the two pizzas. Next, add the spinach leaves; two cups to each pizza. Top with mozzarella cheese and the buffalo mozzarella. Sprinkle the crushed red pepper flakes over the cheeses. Top with the fresh tomato quarters and drizzle tops of pizzas with a little olive oil. Sprinkle with Parmesan cheese. Bake pizzas for about 15 to 18 minutes. Remove from oven and add basil leaves if desired. Makes 2 (14-inch) pizzas.

Time: 2½ Hours

SICILIAN SAUSAGE PIZZA

Note: *Pizza is always a treat, and homemade is even better. You will love all the Italian flavor in this old favorite.*

1 recipe **Basic Pizza Dough**, found on page 119

1 recipe **Rosalie's Marinara Sauce**, found on page 160

2 (14-inch) pizza stones

2 tablespoons cornmeal, divided

Olive oil

1 pound sweet Italian sausage

2 tablespoons olive oil, divided

2½ cups prepared marinara sauce, divided

1 cup Parmesan cheese, divided

1 cup sliced mushrooms, divided

1 cup sun-dried tomatoes, divided

1 cup black olives, divided, optional

1 cup shredded mozzarella cheese, divided

Fresh basil

Crushed red pepper flakes

Grated Parmesan cheese

1. Preheat oven to 425 degrees. Prepare pizza dough as instructed for
    two pizzas. Place the pizza dough on pizza stones, and continue to roll or
    stretch until the circle is to the edge of the stone. Place cornmeal below the
    pizza dough. Let dough rise for at least 30 minutes while preparing topping.

2. Pour about 2 tablespoons olive oil in fry pan; add sausage. Fry sausage over
    medium heat until partially cooked; crumble and set aside.

3. Brush 1 tablespoon olive oil over each pizza dough. Pour 1¼ cups marinara sauce over
    the olive oil and spread evenly over the dough.

4. Sprinkle ½ cup Parmesan cheese over the marinara. Place ½ cup mushroom slices over
    the cheese. Add ½ cup sun-dried tomatoes. Next, add ½ cup olives, if using. Sprinkle ½
    cup shredded mozzarella cheese over the pizza. Garnish with loose basil leaves, and red
    pepper flakes.

5. Bake pizzas for 15 to 18 minutes, or until browned underneath and bubbly on top.
    Makes 2 pizzas.

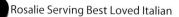

Rosalie Serving Best Loved Italian

PASTA & SAUCE DISHES

Let's Cook Pasta

What would the Italian cuisine be without pasta? It is, and always has been, the main dish one thinks about when talking about Italian food. When I grew up, my mother would make pasta dishes about three to four times a week. She would cook it up with cauliflower, broccoli, and greens (like spinach and tomatoes), and even beans. She would put tiny "acini de pepe" in her meatball soup, and even fry left over mostaccioli in the skillet with olive oil. On special occasions, she would make homemade pasta, homemade ravioli, and even homemade gnocchi dumplings.

When folks popped in unannounced, she could boil up a pound of angel hair in 5 minutes. She would add some chopped garlic, fresh basil, and with her extra virgin olive oil and fresh grated Romano cheese, we had dinner!

Many of the pasta recipes in this section are the very ones that I grew up with. Some of them are simple and quick, with dinner was on the table as easy as boiling angel hair! Others may take a little time, but were always worth the effort. Now let me give you a few tips for the perfect pasta:

1. Always cook pasta in a large deep pot, so the noodles do not stick to one another. Use a generous amount water, and only add the pasta when the water is boiling. Choose a good brand of pasta; I love Barilla.

2. Salt the water with at least 1 tablespoon of salt, which will bring out the flavor of the pasta. Taste the pasta about 2 minutes into boiling, and add a little more salt if needed.

3. Never rinse pasta with water. The starch on the noodles is necessary to adhere to the sauce, thus "marrying" noodles and sauce. The only exception to this would be to cool down lasagna noodles, leaving some of the original pasta water in the bottom of the pot, in order to handle the noodles.

4. Never add olive oil to the boiling water. Again, we want the starch to stay on the pasta.

5. Cook the pasta to "al dente" and no longer. Al dente means "to the tooth", which means that when you take a bite of the cooked pasta, it will actually stick to your teeth. It would be better to have the pasta a little undercooked, than gummy. Remember, pasta continues to cook when added to the hot sauce.

6. If you are making oil sauces, you can lift the pasta right out of the boiling water with a spaghetti spoon and into your pasta bowl. This gives the dish a little of the pasta water, and helps to extend the sauce. When making these sauces, always keep back a cup or more of your pasta water, especially if the pasta becomes dry. The starchy water is full of flavor and has revived many pasta dishes.

7. If at all possible, serve the warm pasta as soon as possible for the best flavor.

Time: 1½ Hours

ROSALIE'S SUNDAY RED SAUCE OVER PENNE

Note: *This is the red sauce that I grew up with, and it maybe the best pasta sauce you will ever experience. Made with savory meat and fennel meatballs, it is rich and delicious. This recipe makes a good amount, enough for up to 8 people, and it also freezes very well for future use.*

1 recipe **Italian Meatballs** on page 172

1 pound penne pasta

1 tablespoon salt

¼ cup olive oil

1 small onion, chopped

1 (15-ounce) can diced tomatoes with juice

3 teaspoons sugar

1 teaspoon dried basil leaves

½ teaspoon salt

¼ teaspoon ground black pepper

1 cup Kitchen Basics Chicken stock

2 (29-ounce) cans tomato sauce

3 (6-ounce) cans tomato paste

1 large chicken breast with rib bone

1 pound country-style ribs, cut into 4-inch pieces

Lawry's coarse garlic salt

2 Italian mild sausage links

Olive oil, divided

Parmesan grated cheese

1. In an 8-quart heavy pot, sauté onion in olive oil until translucent and slightly golden, about 2 minutes. Add the tomatoes, sugar, basil leaves, salt, and pepper. Allow the tomatoes and spices to come to a steady soft boil. Cook over medium heat about 6 to 8 minutes.

2. Add the chicken stock, tomato sauce, and tomato paste. Rinse tomato cans with a little water and add to the sauce. Stir the pot well to break up the tomato paste. Cover with lid and simmer over low heat.

3. Rinse the chicken breast in cool water and pat dry. Prepare the ribs in the same way. Sprinkle both chicken and ribs liberally with the coarse garlic salt. Fry chicken and ribs in skillet with olive oil for about 6 to 8 minutes on each side; add to the sauce. Brown the sausage in the same skillet, using more olive oil as needed. Cut the sausage into 2-inch pieces and add to the sauce. Sausage should not be cooked through, just browned.

4. Prepare the meatballs according to recipe instructions. Pour olive oil in skillet, enough to cover bottom of pan. Lightly brown meatballs on all sides; do not cook through. Add the meatballs to the sauce and continue to cook until the sauce and the other meats are done, usually about 1 hour. Keep lid on pot and cook on low heat, stirring often to avoid sauce burning on bottom of pan.

5. Boil penne pasta in an 8-quart pot of salted water until al dente. Do not overcook pasta. Drain pasta and place in large pasta bowl; add sauce and serve. Pass Parmesan cheese for garnish. Serves 8.

Time: 1 Hour

BAKED RIGATONI WITH
SAUSAGE & RED/CREAM SAUCE

Note: *This baked pasta is wonderful, warm, and rich with cheeses. It has a homemade marinara sauce and lots of Italian sausage with every bite. Everyone will love this dish.*

1 recipe **Rosalie's Marinara Sauce**, found on page 160

1 (16-ounce) package rigatoni

1 tablespoon salt

2 tablespoon olive oil

1 pound ground sweet Italian sausage

4 cups homemade marinara sauce, divided

⅓ cup heavy whipping cream

⅔ cup Pecorino Romano, divided

2 cups rope Provel cheese, or 4 slices Provolone

½ cup shaved Parmesan cheese

1. Preheat oven to 350 degrees. Prepare marinara sauce according to recipe and place in medium 6-quart saucepan; set aside. In large skillet, pour in olive oil and sauté sausage over medium heat for 6 minutes; sausage should be partially cooked. Add the crumbled sausage to the marinara sauce, and continue to simmer together for about 10 minutes.

2. Boil rigatoni in boiling water with salt added for 10 to 12 minutes, keeping the rigatoni firm to the bite; do not overcook. Drain rigatoni and place into large bowl. Add all but 1 cup of the marinara sauce, and add the heavy cream; stir well.

3. Using an olive oil spray, coat the bottom of a 9x13-inch pan. Place half of the rigatoni in pan and then sprinkle ⅓ cup Pecorino Romano cheese over the pasta. Place other half of rigatoni over cheese and top the rigatoni with the other ⅓ cup Pecorino Romano. Next add the remaining 1 cup marinara sauce over rigatoni. Lay the provolone cheese over the sauce and sprinkle with shaved Parmesan cheese. Cover rigatoni with aluminum foil and bake covered for 15 minutes. Remove foil and place back in oven to melt cheese on top if not fully melted. Serve with Italian bread sticks. Makes 8 to 10 servings.

Time: 30 Minutes

SAUSAGE & PEPPER SAUCE WITH ROTINI

Note: *If you like peppers and sausage, you will love this dish. It is simple and delicious to make and a great dish when pressed for time.*

1 pound rotini

1 tablespoon salt

3 bell peppers, green, yellow, red, or mixed

¼ to ⅓ cup extra virgin olive oil

½ onion, chopped, about ½ cup

2 cloves garlic, chopped

½ teaspoon salt

¼ teaspoon ground black pepper

2 Italian sausage links, cut into 2-inch rounds

1 (15-ounce) can tomato sauce

1 teaspoon sugar

½ teaspoon dried basil leaves

¼ teaspoon crushed red pepper flakes

¼ cup Kitchen Basics chicken stock

Salt and pepper

½ cup reserved pasta water

Freshly grated Parmesan

Coarse ground black pepper

1. Wash, core and seed peppers; cut in julienne pieces, not too thin. Place peppers in saucepan with olive oil, onion, and garlic. Sprinkle salt and pepper over the peppers as they fry. Add sausage and sauté until peppers are tender and sausage is cooked, about 8 to 10 minutes.

2. Add tomato sauce, sugar, basil, crushed red pepper flakes, chicken stock, salt, and pepper to taste. Simmer sauce on low heat, about 15 minutes.

3. Boil rotini in an 8-quart pot of boiling water with salt added for about 7 minutes. Drain rotini, and reserve ½ cup pasta water. Place rotini with the reserved pasta water into a large pasta bowl. Add the sauce and toss together until well blended. Sprinkle with Parmesan cheese and coarse black pepper. Serves 6 to 8.

Time: 1 Hour

BAKED LASAGNA
WITH ROSALIE'S MEAT SAUCE

Note: *Baked Lasagna is the ever popular layered noodles, and can be made in many ways. Some prefer a vegetable lasagna, seafood, or as below, with a meat sauce. It is easy to interchange, and always a delicious dish.*

1 recipe **Rosalie's Meat Sauce**
found on page 158

9 Barilla Lasagna sheets

1 tablespoon salt

1 (15-ounce) container ricotta cheese

2 tablespoon fresh curly parsley,
chopped fine

½ cup grated Parmesan cheese

1 egg

Salt and pepper

1 (16-ounce) bag shredded mozzarella,
divided, or 4 cups Italian cheese blend

½ cup grated Parmesan

1. Preheat oven to 350 degrees. Prepare meat sauce as directed; set aside. Boil lasagna in an 8-quart pot of boiling water with salt added, about 10 to 12 minutes.

2. While lasagna is cooking, make the ricotta filling by placing ricotta in a medium bowl. Add the parsley, Parmesan cheese, egg, salt, and pepper to taste. Using a whisk, mix the ricotta with seasonings until fully combined. When the lasagna is cooked al dente, re-move pot and drain all but about 2 cups water. Add 4 cups cool water in order to handle the noodles.

3. Using a 9x13 pan, pour 1 cup sauce on bottom of pan without meat. Layer 3 lasagna sheets over the sauce. Dollop ½ of the ricotta over the sheets and 1 cup shredded moz-zarella over the ricotta. Next add 1½ cups sauce. Repeat the layer again using ricotta, cheese and sauce. Top the third layer with 3 more lasagna sheets, and add about 2 cups sauce. Top with grated Parmesan and more of the shredded mozzarella. Cover with foil and bake for 35 to 40 minutes, or until bubbly and cheese is melted on top. Remove from oven and let sit for at least 15 minutes. Makes 12 servings.

William & Ann Fiorino

Time: 50 Minutes

SPINACH LASAGNA ROLL-UPS

Note: *These lasagna roll-ups are very easy to make and can take the place of manicotti without the work of stuffing. They are delicious with your favorite marinara or meat sauce.*

1 recipe **Rosalie's Marinara Sauce** on page 160
   or **Rosalie's Meat Sauce** on page 158

12 lasagna sheets

1 tablespoon salt

3 cups ricotta cheese

3 cups shredded mozzarella, divided
   or 5-cheese Italian

1½ cups Pecorino Romano cheese, divided

2 eggs, beaten

2 tablespoons fresh curly parsley, chopped

½ teaspoon salt

¼ teaspoon ground black pepper

1 (8-ounce) package fresh baby spinach

1 small clove garlic, minced

1 tablespoon extra-virgin olive oil

Crushed red pepper flakes, optional

Fresh basil leaves

1.   Preheat oven to 350 degrees. Prepare marinara sauce, or meat
     sauce; set aside. Boil lasagna sheets in an 8-quart pot of boil-
     ing water with salt added, for about 8 to 9 minutes. While lasagna
     is cooking, make the ricotta cheese filling by placing the ricotta in a
     large bowl. Add 2 cups shredded mozzarella and ¾ cup Pecorino Romano
     cheese and mix the ricotta and cheeses together. Add the eggs, parsley, salt,
     and pepper to the mixture and mix in well.

2.   Sauté the spinach and garlic in olive oil over medium heat, just until wilted and flavored;
     chop spinach small. Fold the spinach into the ricotta mixture.

3.   When lasagna sheets are cooked al dente, pour off all but 2 cups boiling water. Add 4 cups

cool water to the pot in order to handle sheets. Prepare a 9x13 baking pan by pouring 1 cup sauce on bottom of pan. If using meat sauce, omit meat on bottom of pan for easier placement of the roll-ups. Remove 1 lasagna sheet at a time and lay on cutting board. Dollop about ⅓ cup of the ricotta mixture over the noodle, and roll up jelly-roll style. Place the rolled up lasagna sheet seam-side down in the pan. Continue with the other sheets until all are arranged in the baking pan. Add 2½ to 3 cups sauce over roll-ups. Sprinkle the remaining mozzarella and Pecorino Romano cheese over the sauce. Garnish top with red pepper flakes if desired. Cover with foil, and bake in oven for 30 minutes, or until bubbly and cheese is melted on top. Remove from oven and let sit 15 minutes.

4. Place 2 roll-ups on a plate and garnish top with fresh basil leaves. Serves 6.

Time: 45 Minutes

HOMEMADE PASTA DOUGH

Note: *Many times during the Christmas holidays, my son Jeff will make this pasta right on the kitchen table.*
We get down the pasta machine and everyone stands around and watches the ribbons of noodles parade out onto the table.
When cooked, they almost melt in your mouth, as homemade pasta is very light and tender.

1½ cups all-purpose flour

2 eggs

1. There are only two ingredients you need to make an excellent pasta dough. It may be necessary on occasion to add a bit of warm water to form a workable dough if the liquid content of the egg is low or the absorption balance of the flour is high. Use the dip-and-sweep method for measuring the flour. Dip the measuring cup into the flour and sweep it off with the straight edge of a knife. Clear off the table, or use a large counter space to work the dough.

2. Form a well with a knife or your fingers to hold the eggs. Keep the sides high to prevent the eggs from running out of the well. Drop the eggs into the center of the well. Scramble the eggs with a fork and start to pick up the flour from inside the well with the fork, incorporating the flour into the eggs gradually until the eggs are no longer runny.

3. At this point you must use your hands. Bring all the flour from the outside of the well into the center. Form the entire mass into a ball. Use the excess flour outside the ball only if the dough feels wet. In that case, bring it in gradually as needed to form a soft but not sticky ball of dough. Pick up the ball of dough and squeeze it firmly between your hands while rotating it.

4. Now, the kneading process. Push down on the dough firmly, with the heel of your hand pushing into the center of the dough. Give the dough quarter turns while you are kneading. If the dough sticks to your hand, dust it with flour and continue kneading. A 2-egg recipe generally requires 8 to 10 minutes of kneading. Your objective is to finish with a ball of dough that is smooth and satiny but not tough.

5. Roll out the pasta dough on a lightly floured surface and cut the dough into six or eight pieces. Working with one piece at a time, fashion each piece into a rough rectangle, then pass it through your pasta machine on the widest setting (usually #1). Fold dough in half or in thirds and pass it through again. Then fold and pass it through one more time. Continue passing the dough through the machine, possibly 6 to 8 times until the dough feels smooth and satiny, closing down the opening of the rollers a few notches with each pass, and dusting them very lightly with flour if the dough is sticking, until you have reached the desired thickness. Cover the remaining dough parts with a damp towel to prevent them from drying out. Then, if you wish to make fettuccine or spaghetti, use the pasta cutter attachment to cut the sheets into the desired thickness, or cut the pasta by hand on the counter top with a chef's knife to whatever size strands or shapes you want.

6.   Boil pasta an 8-quart pot of boiling water with 1 tablespoon salt added. Fresh pasta cooks in much less time than ready-made pasta; at times, no more than 3 to 4 minutes. Be careful not to overcook pasta, check often for al dente.

7.   7. Once you get the hang of making fresh pasta, you will have so much fun doing it, and you definitely will love the fresh cooked delicacy. Makes about 8 ounces pasta noodles. Serves 2 to 4. **NOTE:** This recipe is taken from the book *Pasta Tecnica*, and taught by author *Pasquale Bruno, Jr.*

CELEBRATING

FAMILY

Time: 1 Hour and 15 Minutes

STUFFED JUMBO SHELLS WITH SPINACH RICOTTA

Note: *These stuffed shells are absolutely wonderful. Served with Italian salad and bread, it makes for a great dinner menu.*

Rosalie's Marinara Sauce recipe found on page 160

Rosalie's Italian Meatballs recipe found on page 172, optional

½ package jumbo shells, about 20

1 tablespoon salt

9x13-inch glass baking dish

Olive oil to brush pan

1 (15-ounce) container ricotta cheese

2 cups shredded mozzarella cheese, divided

1 cup grated Romano cheese, divided

1 egg, beaten

1 tablespoon fresh curly parsley, chopped

½ teaspoon salt

½ teaspoon ground black pepper

2 cups fresh baby spinach, packed

1 small clove garlic, minced

1 tablespoon olive oil

1. Preheat oven to 350 degrees. Prepare the marinara sauce. If using the Italian meatballs, brown, crumble, and add to sauce. Simmer together about 15 minutes. Boil jumbo shells in 8-quart pot with salt added. Shells should be a little undercooked, to accommodate baking time.

2. While shells are cooking, mix together ricotta cheese filling by placing ricotta in a large bowl. Add 1½ cups mozzarella and ½ cup Parmesan cheese. Mix the ricotta and cheeses together. Add the egg, parsley, salt, and pepper to the mixture, mix together until combined.

3. Sauté the spinach and garlic in olive oil over medium heat, just until wilted and flavored; chop spinach small. Fold the spinach into the ricotta mixture.

4. When shells are cooked about 10-12 minutes, pour off all but 2 cups water. Add 4 cups cool water to the pot in order to handle shells. Prepare a 9x13-inch baking pan by pouring 1 to 1½ cups of sauce over the bottom. Remove one shell at a time and stuff the shell with about 1 heaping tablespoon ricotta filling. Arrange the shells over the sauce and top shells with another 2 cups, or more sauce. Sprinkle remaining mozzarella and Parmesan cheese over top. Cover with foil and bake for 30 minutes. Remove from oven and let sit for 15 minutes. Makes 8 to 10 servings.

Time: 20 Minutes

PASTA WITH CAULIFLOWER

Note: *This is a quick pasta, as we would call it growing up. It was always a welcome dish, with lots of tender cauliflower and tomatoes.*

1 (12-ounce) package mini rotini,
or 12-ounces angel hair

1 tablespoon salt

¼ cup olive oil

½ cup onion, chopped

2 cloves garlic, chopped

2 cups cauliflower florets

½ teaspoon salt

½ teaspoon ground black pepper

2 fresh tomatoes, cored and quartered
or 1 (15-ounce) can diced tomatoes,
juice included

5 to 6 fresh basil leaves, chopped
or ½ teaspoon dried basil leaves

1 teaspoon sugar

Salt and pepper

1 tablespoon extra-virgin olive oil

½ reserved pasta water

Freshly grated Parmesan cheese

Freshly ground black pepper

1. Pour olive oil in a large skillet and add onion, garlic, and cauliflower; stir-fry over medium heat for 10 to 12 minutes. Salt and pepper cauliflower while frying, and stir often.

2. Add tomatoes, basil, sugar, salt, and pepper to taste. Simmer the tomatoes and cauliflower together about 8 minutes on low heat.

3. Boil pasta in an 8-quart pot of boiling water with 1 tablespoon salt added for no more than 3 to 4 minutes. When pasta is al dente, drain rotini reserving 1 cup pasta water. If using angel hair, lift the pasta right out of the pot with a spaghetti spoon and place it into the pan with the sauce. Add the tablespoon olive oil and ½ cup reserved pasta water. Toss the pasta with the sauce, and transfer pasta to a large pasta bowl. Garnish with Parmesan cheese and freshly ground black pepper. Makes 6 servings.

Rosalie Serving Best Loved Italian

Time: 15 Minutes

PASTA WITH FRESH TOMATOES & BASIL

Note: *This dish could be my signature dish because I have made it so many times. It is the simplest dish to make, and so good, one could easily become addicted. The secret is to make it with fresh ingredients, and serve it immediately.*

1 pound angel hair or vermicelli

1 tablespoon salt

2 large vine-ripened tomatoes, cored and chopped

½ cup extra virgin olive oil

3 cloves garlic, chopped fine

2 cups fresh basil leaves, torn small

1 teaspoon coarse sea salt

¼ teaspoon coarse ground black pepper

¼ teaspoon crushed red pepper flakes

½ cup reserved pasta water

Freshly grated Parmesan cheese

1. Place tomatoes in large pasta bowl and add the olive oil, garlic, basil leaves, salt, pepper, and crushed red pepper flakes; toss together well and set aside.

2. Boil pasta in an 8-quart pot of boiling water with salt added. Add the angel hair and boil 3 to 4 minutes; do not overcook. Pasta should be al dente. Using a spaghetti spoon, lift the pasta right out of the water and put it into the pasta bowl with tomato/basil sauce; add the ½ cup reserved pasta water. Toss together well, and sprinkle with the Parmesan cheese. Serves 6.

Time: 15 Minutes

Spaghetti Aglio é Olio

Note: *This pasta, also known as **Spaghetti with Garlic and Oil**, is a longtime favorite in almost every Italian home. I can guarantee every Italian child grew up with this dish. We had it at least once a week, and I can still smell the garlic.*

1 pound thin spaghetti

1 tablespoon salt

¾ cup extra virgin olive oil

3 cloves garlic, chopped fine

⅓ cup fresh basil leaves, chopped

Coarse sea salt

Freshly ground black pepper

½ cup freshly grated Parmesan cheese

Pour olive oil into a large pasta bowl. Add the garlic and basil and stir together. Boil pasta in an 8-quart pot of boiling water with salt added. Angel hair cooks very fast, about 3 to 4 minutes; do not overcook. When pasta is cooked al dente, lift the pasta right out of the water and into the pasta bowl with the olive oil. Add about ½ to 1 cup reserved pasta water. Add the salt and pepper to taste and toss together well. Garnish top with Parmesan cheese. Serves 4 to 6.

Taylor & Gia

Time: 25 Minutes

Angel Hair with Garlic, Spinach, & Marinara

Note: *This dish is a dream on a night when you need to make something quick.
It is absolutely delicious with lots of spinach paired with angel hair and marinara.*

1 pound angel hair pasta

1 tablespoon salt

¼ cup extra virgin olive oil

2 to 3 cloves garlic, chopped fine

1 (15-ounce) can diced tomatoes

1 (8-ounce) can tomato sauce

½ teaspoon dried basil

½ teaspoon sugar

Sprinkle of salt and pepper

¼ teaspoon crushed red pepper flakes

1 chicken bouillon cube

1 (10-ounce) package baby spinach

⅓ cup extra virgin olive oil

1 cup hot pasta water

Parmesan cheese

Coarse black pepper

1. Put water on to boil with salt added. Prepare the marinara by pouring olive oil into a medium saucepan. Add the garlic to the olive oil and sizzle only for 30 seconds; do not brown the garlic. Add the diced tomatoes, tomato sauce, basil, sugar, salt, and pepper. Bring the sauce to a gentle boil; add the crushed red pepper flakes and bouillon cube. Let sauce simmer for about 6 to 8 minutes.

2. Cook the angel hair in the boiling salted water for only about 3 to 4 minutes. While pasta is cooking, place the spinach into a large pasta bowl. When pasta is done al dente, lift it right out of the pasta water with a spaghetti spoon and onto the spinach; this will wilt the spinach nicely. Next, add the olive oil and pasta water. Pour the marinara sauce over the pasta and toss evenly. Sprinkle about ¼ cup Parmesan cheese over the top. Garnish with coarse black pepper. Serves 6.

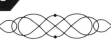
Time: 30 Minutes

ANGEL HAIR FLORENTINE

Note: *You will love how pretty this dish looks on your table. It has all the colors of Italy, red, green, and white, and is an all-time favorite.*

1 (12-ounce) package angel hair pasta

1 tablespoon salt

2 skinless chicken breasts

Lawry's coarse ground garlic salt with parsley added

¼ cup olive oil

5 to 6 cloves garlic, chopped fine

¾ cup extra virgin olive oil, divided

1 (10-ounce) bag fresh spinach

1 cup grape tomatoes

1 cup reserved pasta water

Coarse sea salt

Fresh ground black pepper

1 cup Parmesan cheese

1. Rinse chicken breasts in cold water and pat dry; cut away any fat or gristle. Sprinkle both sides with the garlic salt and fry in olive oil in skillet for 10 to 12 minutes, turning once or twice. Put lid on pan and steam chicken for 2 minutes longer. Cool, and cut into small pieces; set aside.

2. Add chopped garlic to ¾ cup olive in large saucepan, enough to hold both sauce and pasta. Heat gently about 30 seconds, or until light golden. Add the spinach, tomatoes, and chicken. Stir together until heated through, about 3 minutes.

3. Boil pasta in an 8-quart pot of boiling water with salt added. Cook angel hair 3 to 4 minutes; do not overcook. Using a spaghetti spoon, lift pasta right out of the water into the pan with sauce. Add 1 cup of the reserved pasta water. Toss pasta with spinach/chicken until well coated. Add salt and pepper to taste.

4. Transfer pasta to a large pasta bowl and garnish with Parmesan cheese, and more ground black pepper. Serves 6.

Time: 20 Minutes

BROCCOLI RABE WITH GARLIC LINGUINE

Note: *Broccoli Rabe is a vegetable that is both related to the cabbage and turnip families. It is a bundle of stalks with scattered clusters of tiny broccoli-like buds. This type of broccoli is often paired with a light oil sauce and lots of chopped garlic and seasonings.*

12 ounces linguine

1 tablespoon salt

1 pound broccoli rabe, trimmed

3 tablespoons extra virgin olive oil, divided

1 tablespoon butter

3 cloves garlic, finely chopped

½ teaspoon salt

¼ teaspoon ground black pepper

¼ teaspoon crushed red pepper flakes

½ cup Kitchen Basics chicken stock

Reserved pasta water

Parmesan cheese

Freshly ground black pepper

1. Boil linguine in an 8-quart pot of boiling water with salt added according to package directions, about 10 minutes. Trim ¼-inch off the bottoms of broccoli rabe stems; discard coarse outer leaves. Rinse broccoli rabe in cold water and cut into 2-inch pieces; set aside.

2. In large skillet, sauté the garlic in 2 tablespoons oil and butter for about 30 seconds. Add the broccoli rabe, salt and pepper, and the red pepper flakes. Add the chicken stock and simmer on medium heat for about 4 to 5 minutes, or until broccoli rabe is tender.

3. When linguine is cooked al dente, lift the pasta right out of the boiling water with a spaghetti spoon, and place it into the skillet with the broccoli rabe. Add the remaining 1 tablespoon olive oil and ½ to 1 cup of the reserved pasta water to extend the sauce. Remove pasta to a large pasta bowl and garnish top with grated Parmesan cheese and freshly ground black pepper. Serves 6.

Time: 25 Minutes

SPAGHETTI ALLA CARBONARA

Note: *Spaghetti alla Carbonara was a discovery in the 1970s, when Americans first realized that pasta could be dressed with cream sauce as well as red. The craze was overwhelming, and the cream sauces took flight. This dish is scrumptious and is rich in eggs, cream, and bacon. If you don't have pancetta, regular bacon can be used.*

1 pound spaghetti

1 tablespoon salt

4 slices pancetta cut into 1-inch pieces, or regular bacon

2 tablespoons extra virgin olive oil

4 cloves garlic, chopped fine

2 large eggs, room temperature

1 cup heavy whipping cream

1 cup Parmigiano-Reggiano cheese

½ cup reserved pasta water

Freshly ground black pepper

2 tablespoons fresh curly parsley

1. Preheat oven to 225 degrees. Fry pancetta in olive oil in a large skillet until crisp, about 8 to 10 minutes. Add the garlic and sauté in with the pancetta for 30 seconds. Turn to very low, or turn skillet off.

2. Boil spaghetti in an 8-quart pot of boiling water with salt added according to package directions. While spaghetti is boiling, place a large pasta bowl in the oven to warm (this is important in order to cook the raw eggs.)

3. In medium bowl beat the eggs until lemon colored. Add the cream and the cheese; whip together until smooth and creamy; set aside.

4. When spaghetti is cooked al dente, turn off heat and lift the spaghetti right out of the boiling water with a spaghetti spoon and put it into the skillet with the bacon, garlic, and drippings. Add the reserved pasta water, and stir the spaghetti into the bacon mixture until well coated. Remove the warm bowl out of the oven and place the spaghetti into the warm bowl. Add the egg/cheese/cream mixture onto the spaghetti, and with two forks, toss the spaghetti into the cream until well coated.

5. Garnish with ground black pepper and parsley. Serve while warm and pass extra cheese at the table. Serves 8.

Time: 20 Minutes

VERMICELLI WITH PEAS & PANCETTA

Note: *This is a delightful pasta dish with a creamy sauce and frozen peas and mushrooms. Even people who don't like peas usually love this dish. If you cannot get pancetta, use regular bacon.*

12 ounces vermicelli

1 tablespoon salt

4 to 5 slices pancetta, or lean sliced bacon

4 tablespoons extra virgin olive oil, divided

1 medium onion chopped fine, about 1 cup

2 cups thick-sliced white button mushrooms

½ teaspoon coarse sea salt

½ teaspoon coarse ground black pepper

¼ teaspoon crushed red pepper flakes

3 cups heavy cream

2 cups Pecorino Romano or Parmesan cheese

1 (10-ounce) package frozen peas

1 cup reserved pasta water, divided

1. Fry pancetta in large skillet in 2 tablespoons olive oil until crisp, about 8 to 10 minutes. Move pancetta to edge of skillet and add the onions and mushrooms with another 2 tablespoons olive oil. Sauté together for about 5 minutes until onions and mushrooms are lightly browned. Add the salt, pepper, and crushed red pepper flakes and stir until seasoned.

2. Add the heavy cream and 1 cup of cheese at a time, and stir constantly for about 2 to 3 minutes, until sauce is just bubbly. Turn heat to very low, or remove from heat to avoid burning cream.

3. Boil vermicelli in an 8-quart pot of boiling water with salt added for about 6 to 7 minutes. During last 2 minutes of boiling, add the peas. Complete cooking the vermicelli to al dente. Reserve 1 cup pasta water and drain pasta and peas together. Add the pasta, peas, and a ½ cup of the pasta water to a large pasta bowl. Pour the sauce over the vermicelli; toss together well. Add remaining pasta water to the dish later if the pasta gets too thick to refresh the sauce. Serves 6.

Time: 45 Minutes

PASTA PRIMAVERA

Note: *Pasta Primavera is always a classic dish on the Italian menu. It is especially good in the summer when the vegetables are fresh and at their peak in flavor.*

1 pound rigatoni or shells
or 12 ounces spaghetti

1 tablespoon salt

⅓ cup extra virgin olive oil

1 small onion, chopped

3 cloves garlic, chopped

1 small zucchini, unpeeled and
sliced ¼-inch rounds

1 large bell pepper, yellow or red,
cut into strips

⅔ cup cauliflower florets

⅔ cup broccoli florets,

½ cup asparagus, hard stems trimmed,
cut into thirds, optional

1 teaspoon salt

½ teaspoon ground black pepper

1 15-ounce can tomato sauce

½ teaspoon sugar

½ teaspoon dried basil

¼ teaspoon crushed red pepper flakes

½ cup cherry or grape tomatoes, halved

½ cup reserved pasta water

2 tablespoons extra virgin olive oil

Freshly grated Parmesan cheese

Freshly ground coarse black pepper

Basil sprigs

1. Pour olive oil into a large skillet. Add the onion, garlic, zucchini, bell pepper, cauliflower, broccoli, and asparagus. Stir-fry the vegetables over medium heat until crisp-tender, 8 to 10 minutes. Salt and pepper the vegetables as they fry.

2. Add tomato sauce, sugar, basil, and crushed red pepper flakes. Cook 5 to 6 minutes longer. Add the cherry tomatoes and put vegetables on very low heat, just enough to keep warm.

3. Boil pasta in an 8-quart pot of boiling water with salt added. Cook al dente according to package directions. Reserve ½ cup pasta water and drain pasta.

4. Transfer the pasta to a large pasta platter; add the reserved pasta water and 2 tablespoons olive oil. Add the vegetables and toss together to combine pasta and vegetables. Sprinkle with Parmesan and the ground black pepper. Garnish with basil sprigs. Serves 6 to 8.

Time: 30 Minutes

ROSALIE'S PASTA CON BROCCOLI

Note: *I must admit putting an American touch on this dish by using the Velveeta. I used it once to thicken the sauce a little and loved it so much that I made it a part of the recipe. This dish could be one of the most popular in the Italian-American cuisine. Refrigerate leftovers and add a little milk while re-heating to loosen sauce.*

1 pound shell pasta	1 teaspoon coarse sea salt
1 tablespoon salt	¼ teaspoon coarse ground black pepper
¼ stick butter	4 cups heavy whipping cream
¼ cup extra virgin olive oil	3½ cups grated Parmesan cheese
3 cloves garlic, chopped	1 ounce Velveeta cheese,
3 cups broccoli florets	regular not light
2 cups white capped button mushrooms, sliced thick	Freshly ground coarse black pepper

1. Boil shells in an 8-quart pot of boiling water with salt added.

2. While shells are cooking, melt butter and olive oil in a large skillet. Add garlic, broccoli, mushrooms, salt, and pepper. Stir-fry over medium heat 5 to 6 minutes for crisp-tender vegetables.

3. Add the cream and continue to stir until heated through, 2 to 3 minutes. Add the cheese 1 cup at a time, stirring slowly after each addition of cheese until the cheese is fully melted into the cream. Add the Velveeta and stir in gently until fully melted. Keep heat on low and stir often, or completely remove from heat.

4. When shells are cooked al dente, drain quickly and place in a large pasta bowl. Pour the sauce over the shells. Toss together until well combined. Garnish with freshly ground coarse black pepper and serve while warm. Serves 6 to 8.

Time: 20 Minutes

FETTUCCINE ALFREDO WITH MODIGA GARNISH

Note: This dish is an all-time favorite, and very easy to make. The sauce will seem too much at first, but the pasta will take it up and be very creamy.

1 pound fettuccine

1 tablespoon salt

4 tablespoons butter

1 tablespoon extra-virgin olive oil

3 cloves garlic, chopped

4 cups heavy whipping cream, room temperature

3½ cups grated Parmesan cheese

1 ounce regular Velveeta cheese

1 tablespoon fresh curly parsley, chopped

Coarse ground black pepper

Modiga Garnish

1 tablespoon extra-virgin olive oil

1 clove garlic, finely chopped

½ cup plain bread crumbs

1. Boil fettuccine in an 8-quart pot of boiling water with salt added. While fettuccine is cooking, melt butter with olive oil over low heat in large skillet or large saucepan. Add garlic and heat gently, about 30 seconds. Add cream and continue to stir until heated through.

2. Add the Parmesan cheese, 1 cup at a time, stirring slowly into the sauce. Add the Velveeta cheese, parsley, and pepper to taste. Stir gently until cheeses are fully melted and blended together. Keep the sauce on very low heat, or remove, as the sauce can burn easily.

3. Make the toasted bread crumbs by heating olive oil in small skillet. Add the chopped garlic and sauté about 15 seconds. Add bread crumbs all at once, stirring constantly until crumbs become toasted, about 1 to 2 minutes. Remove from pan into small bowl; set aside.

4. When fettuccine is cooked al dente, lift it right out of water with a spaghetti spoon, and put it directly into saucepan with sauce. Toss together until well coated. Transfer fettuccine to large pasta platter. Garnish the fettuccine with the toasted crumbs. Serves 6.

PASTA & SAUCE DISHES

Time: 20 Minutes

CLASSIC FETTUCCINE ALFREDO

Note: *Visiting Alfredo's in downtown Chicago, I was so happy to be sitting at a table close to where Fettuccine Alfredo was being made fresh, right on the spot. This is the classic recipe.*

1 pound fettuccine

1 tablespoon salt

2 tablespoons butter

2 eggs

1 cup heavy whipping cream, room temperature

1 cup Parmesan cheese

Salt and pepper

Freshly ground coarse black pepper

Freshly grated Parmesan cheese

1. Preheat oven to 225 degrees. Boil fettuccine in an 8-quart pot of boiling water with salt added. While fettuccine is cooking, warm a large pasta bowl in the oven for about 5 minutes.

2. Remove the pasta bowl; set aside. Warm the butter in a small saucepan on very low heat, until the butter turns golden, about 5 minutes. Crack the eggs in the warm bowl and immediately start beating eggs. Add the cream and beat into the eggs; the eggs and cream will become thick. Add the cheese, butter, a little salt and pepper to taste, and continue to stir in together.

3. When fettuccine is cooked al dente, use a spaghetti spoon and lift the pasta right out of the water into the pasta bowl. Toss the pasta with the cream mixture. Garnish with freshly ground black pepper and Parmesan cheese. Makes 6 servings.

Time: 30 Minutes

ROSALIE'S SEAFOOD FETTUCCINE

Note: *This dish is absolutely scrumptious! It has a creamy Alfredo sauce mixed with vegetables and featuring shrimp, crabmeat, and baby scallops.*

1 pound fettuccine

1 tablespoon salt

¼ stick butter

¼ cup olive oil

3 cloves garlic, finely chopped

3 cups broccoli florets

2 cups white capped mushrooms, thick-sliced

1½ teaspoons salt

½ teaspoon ground black pepper

4 cups heavy cream

3 cups grated Parmesan cheese

2 cups fresh or frozen deveined shrimp, medium size

1½ cups crab meat, fresh or imitation

2 cups rope Provel cheese or shredded provolone

½ cup baby bay scallops, optional

Fresh ground black pepper

1. Boil fettuccine in an 8-quart pot of boiling water with salt added for 12 minutes, al dente. Melt butter in a large skillet; add olive oil, garlic, broccoli, mushrooms, salt, and pepper. Stir-fry over medium heat 3 to 4 minutes; keep vegetables crisp tender.

2. Add the cream and gently stir into the vegetables. Bring the cream to a gentle boil and add the Parmesan cheese, 1 cup at a time until completely combined into the cream. Add the shrimp and crabmeat. Continue to cook together until shrimp is pink, about 2 minutes. Add the rope Provel or the shredded provolone and gently stir into the cream until melted, about 2 minutes. Add the bay scallops right at the end of cooking, and simmer about 2 more minutes. Remove from heat; cream sauce can burn easily.

3. Drain the fettuccine and place in a very large pasta bowl. Add the sauce and toss the pasta into the cream. If sauce is too thick add a little extra cream and stir. Garnish with freshly ground black pepper. Serves 8.

Time: 25 Minutes

BAY SCALLOPS WITH SHRIMP
SCAMPI OVER LINGUINE

Note: *Bay scallops are smaller than sea scallops and are sweeter, and when paired with shrimp scampi, this dish couldn't be more delicious.*

1 pound linguine

1 tablespoon salt

1 pound sea scallops

½ stick sweet cream butter

½ cup Progresso Italian style
  bread crumbs

¼ cup grated Parmesan cheese

2 cloves garlic, chopped small

2 tablespoons fresh curly parsley,
  chopped

⅛ teaspoon paprika

2 tablespoons olive oil

6 tablespoons sweet cream butter,
  divided

4 cloves garlic, chopped small

1 pound medium shrimp,
  peeled and deveined

2 tablespoons fresh curly parsley

½ teaspoon crushed red pepper flakes

Butter, melted

Grated Parmesan cheese

1. Prepare scallops by rinsing in cool water and placing them in drainer. If the scallops have a crescent-shaped muscle to the side of the scallop, cut or pull off and discard. Melt butter and place the butter in a large bowl; add the drained scallops and toss to coat; set aside.

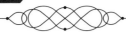
2. Make the breading by combining the bread crumbs, cheese, garlic, parsley and paprika. Place the bread crumb mixture in a large shallow plate. Add the buttered scallops to the bread crumbs and toss to coat.

3. Pour olive oil and 2 tablespoons butter in a large skillet, and add a few of the scallops a little at a time so as not to crowd scallops. Sauté the scallops only 3 to 4 minutes, turning once. Add a little more olive if needed for frying scallops. Remove the scallops to baking sheet; set aside.

4. In same skillet, add the 4 tablespoons remaining butter. Add the garlic and the shrimp. Sauté the garlic and shrimp for only 3 minutes, or until the shrimp turns pink. Add the parsley and red pepper flakes and stir together. Leave the shrimp and garlic in the skillet and add the scallops; gently toss together.

5. Boil linguine in an 8-quart pot of boiling water with salt added. Cook linguine for about 8 to 9 minutes, or until al dente. Lift linguine right out of the boiling water with a spaghetti spoon and place in large pasta bowl. Add 1 cup reserved pasta water. Add the scallops, shrimp and sauce to the pasta, and coat well. Add additional butter if more sauce is desired. Garnish linguine with grated Parmesan cheese. Serves 6.

Time: 15 Minutes

LINGUINE WITH CLAM SAUCE

Note: *Linguine with clam sauce is an old favorite, and a popular dish on the Italian menu. Cheese is not usually served on this particular dish, as it is thought that it interferes with the clams.*

1 pound linguine

1 tablespoon salt

¾ extra virgin olive oil

3 cloves garlic, chopped fine

1 (10-ounce) can whole baby clams, juice included

1 (6.5-ounce) can chopped clams, juice included

⅛ teaspoon dried thyme leaves

¼ teaspoon crushed red pepper flakes

⅔ cup fresh Italian flat-leaf parsley, chopped

Freshly ground black pepper

1. Boil linguine in an 8-quart pot of boiling water with salt added. While pasta is cooking, pour olive oil into saucepan and sauté garlic about 30 seconds, until lightly golden. Add the clams, clam juice, thyme, and crushed red pepper flakes. Simmer together about 5 minutes on low heat. Transfer sauce to a large pasta bowl.

2. Cook the linguine al dente, about 8 to 9 minutes. Using a spaghetti spoon, lift the pasta right out of the boiling water and into the pasta bowl. Add the parsley and toss the linguine until completely coated with the sauce. Garnish top with the freshly ground black pepper. Serves 4 to 6.

Time: 25 Minutes

ANGEL HAIR WITH
LEMON SHRIMP & ASPARAGUS

Note: *You will love this dish with lots of shrimp and a creamy lemon sauce. The asparagus added is a wonderful touch, and compliments the whole dish.*

12 ounces angel hair

1 tablespoon salt

2 tablespoons sweet cream butter

2 tablespoons extra virgin olive oil

1 pound small tender asparagus, ends trimmed and cut into thirds

3 cloves garlic, chopped fine

1 teaspoon coarse sea salt

¼ teaspoon ground black pepper

1 pound fresh, or frozen shrimp, medium size and deveined

¼ teaspoon crushed red pepper flakes

1½ cups half-and-half

2 tablespoon fresh lemon juice

1 teaspoon lemon zest

1 cup Parmesan cheese

Freshly ground black pepper

1. Place butter and olive oil into a large skillet. Add the prepared asparagus with the garlic, salt, and pepper. Sauté over medium heat for 6 to 8 minutes, or until the asparagus is crisp tender.

2. Add the shrimp, crushed red pepper flakes, half-and-half, lemon juice, and lemon zest. Simmer together for about 2 minutes, or until the shrimp turns pink.

3. Transfer sauce to a large pasta bowl. Boil the angel hair in an 8-quart of pot of boiling water with salt added, for only about 3 to 4 minutes, or until al dente. Lift the pasta right out of the boiling water with a spaghetti spoon and into the pasta bowl with sauce; toss together. Add the cheese, and toss again to coat the pasta with the cheese. Garnish with freshly ground black pepper. Serves 4 to 6.

CREAMY MUSHROOM RISOTTO

Note: *This is a classic risotto dish and if you love creamy risotto and mushrooms, you will love this.*
This dish goes so well with your favorite steak or chicken entrée.

7 to 8 cups Kitchen Basics chicken stock

3 tablespoons extra virgin olive oil, divided

4 tablespoons butter, divided

1 pound Portobello mushrooms, thinly sliced and halved

1 pound white button mushrooms, thinly sliced

½ teaspoon sea salt

½ teaspoon freshly ground black pepper

2 cloves garlic, chopped fine

1½ cups Arborio rice

½ cup heavy whipping cream

2 tablespoon green onion tops, finely chopped

1 cup grated Parmesan cheese

1. Pour chicken stock into a medium saucepan and heat to gentle boil. Warm 2 tablespoons olive and 2 tablespoons butter in large skillet over medium-high heat. Stir in the mushrooms, salt, pepper, and garlic, cooking until soft, about 3 minutes. Remove mushrooms and their liquid; set aside.

2. Add the remaining 1 tablespoon olive oil and 2 tablespoons butter to skillet. Over medium heat, add the rice and stir to coat with olive oil and butter, about 2 minutes. When the rice has taken on a pale, golden color, add ½ cup of the hot chicken stock and stir until the stock is absorbed. Continue adding the chicken stock, ½ to 1 cup at a time, stirring continuously, until the liquid is absorbed after each addition. Continue to cook the rice until all the liquid is absorbed and the rice becomes al dente, about 20 to 25 minutes.

3. Remove from heat and stir in the mushrooms with garlic and their liquid. Stir in the cream, green onion tops, and Parmesan cheese. Season with additional salt and pepper to taste. Serves 8.

Time: 3 Hours

HOMEMADE RAVIOLI

Note: *Fresh ravioli is one of those things everyone should experience. Like the homemade pasta, this is a delicious treat.*

4 large fresh eggs

1 teaspoon olive oil

¼ cup water

3 cups all-purpose flour

1 teaspoon salt

1 egg, beaten

1 tablespoon water

1 tablespoon cornmeal

1 recipe **Meat Filling** on page 157

1 recipe **Rosalie's Marinara Sauce** on page 160

1. Prepare meat filling as directed on page 157; set aside. Crack the eggs into a bowl, add the olive oil and water, and beat until fluffy. In a large bowl, mix the flour and salt and make a well in the middle of the flour. Add the egg mixture a little at a time, mixing in some of the flour. Set this mixture to side of bowl. Continue in this manner until the eggs and flour have been used. Continue to bring all the dough together until a ball is formed. Add a little flour if the dough is too sticky to handle. Knead the dough for about 8 minutes, or until the dough is smooth and elastic. Cover the dough ball with a wet towel and let the dough stand for at least 30 minutes to allow the gluten to relax.

2. After the dough has rested, cut the dough into 6 equal pieces, about 4-ounces each. Keep the dough covered with plastic wrap while working with one section of dough at a time. Flatten the section of dough with your hands and flour lightly on both sides. On a lightly flour surface, roll the dough out with a wooden rolling pin, turning often and dusting with flour as needed. Roll the dough very thin into a large rectangle or circle, about 12 to 14 inches. You should see the imprint of your hand through the dough. Beat egg with water until foamy. Brush one-half of the dough lightly with the egg wash. Place the filling by teaspoon size on the brushed half of the dough starting at the top, about 1 inch apart and continue to bottom and to the edge of the dough sheet. Make three rows, about 15 dollops of filling. Take the unbrushed half of the dough, stretching if necessary, and bring it over to cover the filling. Seal the edge with fingers. Press the dough together down the middle of the rows, removing as much air as possible.

3. With a ravioli or pastry cutter, cut the dough down the middle of the rows and then again between each pocket. This should make fifteen 2-inch ravioli. Place on cookie sheet sprinkled with cornmeal and place in freezer if not using immediately. Let freeze until firm, about 10 minutes, then place in a gallon freezer bag until ready for use. Each section of dough should make 12 to 15 ravioli, totaling about 90 ravioli for the entire recipe batch.

4. Boil the ravioli in an 8-quart pot of boiling water with salt added. Drop gently about 10 at a time for 5 minutes. Place the lid on the boiling pot midway to steam the ravioli. Remove gently with slotted spoon, place on large platter.

5. Continue to boil ravioli until you have the desired amount for the servings needed. Dress with marinara. Garnish liberally with freshly grated Parmesan cheese. Entire recipe serves 10 to 12.

Time: 1 Hour

MEAT FILLING FOR HOMEMADE RAVIOLI

Note: *Homemade ravioli can be made with many different fillings. This recipe is very traditional, but any variation of ground meat, spinach, ricotta, or just a combination of cheeses can be used.*

¾ pound ground chuck

¼ pound ground pork

1 teaspoon salt

¼ teaspoon ground black pepper

⅛ teaspoon crushed red pepper flakes

¼ cup olive oil

1 cup Kitchen Basics Chicken Stock

1 egg

1 large clove garlic, minced

¼ cup fresh Italian flat-leaf parsley, chopped fine

½ cup grated Parmesan or Romano cheese

1 to 2 tablespoons plain bread crumbs

1. In a medium bowl, mix the ground chuck, ground pork, salt, pepper, and red pepper flakes until thoroughly mixed together. Brown meat in large deep skillet or saucepan in olive oil until meat is no longer pink. Add the chicken stock and turn the heat to very low. Cook, stirring occasionally and adding more stock if necessary, until the meat is tender and the sauce thickened, about 45 minutes. Remove from heat and let cool.

2. Mix the egg, garlic, parsley, and cheese. Mix the egg mixture and meat mixture together and taste; adding any additional seasoning if desired. Add the bread crumbs if mixture is too moist. Put the mixture in a food processor and pulse 15 to 30 seconds, until the meat is pureed. If food processor is not available, squeeze the meat with your hands several times until the filling comes together in a smooth consistency. Use immediately or freeze for later use. Makes 1 pound filling.

Time: 25 Minutes

ROSALIE'S MEAT SAUCE

Note: *This sauce is so delicious, you will be surprised it only takes a few minutes to prepare.*
Use it in all your favorite pasta dishes, (up to 1 pound of pasta) and in your favorite baked lasagna recipes.
Rinse tomato cans with a little water, about 2 tablespoons, and add to sauce.

1 pound ground chuck or sirloin

2 cloves garlic, chopped

¼ cup plain bread crumbs

¼ cup Parmesan cheese

2 tablespoons fresh curly parsley, chopped

2 eggs

½ teaspoon fennel seed

½ teaspoon salt

¼ teaspoon ground black pepper

Olive oil

¼ cup extra virgin olive oil

1 small onion, chopped small

2 cloves garlic, chopped small

1 (15-ounce) can diced tomatoes

2 teaspoons sugar

½ teaspoon dried basil leaves

¼ teaspoon crushed red pepper flakes,

½ teaspoon salt

¼ teaspoon ground black pepper

1 chicken bouillon cube

½ cup Kitchen Basics chicken stock

1 (15-ounce) can tomato sauce

1 (8-ounce) can tomato paste

½ cup water

1. In large bowl, combine ground chuck, garlic, bread crumbs, cheese, parsley, eggs, fennel seed, salt, and pepper. With clean hands, mix the meat and seasonings well. Place meat in large skillet with enough olive oil to cover bottom of pan. Fry meat on both sides for 3 to 4 minutes, leaving meat partially uncooked. Crumble meat in pan as it cooks. Remove back to bowl and set aside.

2. Prepare the marinara sauce by combining olive oil, onion, and garlic in a 6-quart sauce pan and sauté onions and garlic about 2 to 3 minutes or until golden in color. Add tomatoes, sugar, basil leaves, red pepper flakes, salt, pepper, and bouillon cube; let simmer 5 minutes. Add the chicken stock and bring back to simmer, about 5 more minutes.

3. Add the tomato sauce, and paste and stir well to break up the paste. Add the water, and a little more if needed for a smooth consistency. Let the sauce simmer on low heat about 6 to 8 minutes. Add the partially cooked meat, and let simmer for another 10 minutes. Serve over favorite pasta, or in pasta dishes. Makes 6 cups sauce.

RICOTTA & SPINACH FILLING FOR HOMEMADE RAVIOLI

Note: *This filling is delicious for ravioli and is great served with your favorite marinara sauce.*

1½ cups ricotta cheese

1 cup freshly grated Parmesan cheese

½ shredded mozzarella cheese

1 egg

Salt and pepper to taste

¼ teaspoon nutmeg

2 tablespoons olive oil

1 (10-ounce) bag baby spinach, washed and air-dried

1. In medium bowl, combine ricotta cheese, Parmesan cheese, mozzarella, egg, salt, pepper, and nutmeg; set aside. In large skillet, combine olive oil and spinach. Over medium heat, wilt the spinach until tender, about 2 minutes. Remove and using kitchen scissors, cut spinach small. Fold the spinach into the ricotta mixture.

2. Use filling to fill ravioli pockets. Makes enough filling for 1 recipe *Homemade Ravioli* on page 156.

Sebastian Schultz

Time: 15 Minutes

ROSALIE'S MARINARA SAUCE

Note: *This could be one of the best marinara sauces you have ever tasted. It makes up quick in just 15 minutes, and can be used over pasta, meat entrées and for dips.*

¼ cup extra virgin olive oil

1 small onion, chopped

2 cloves garlic, chopped

1 (15-ounce) can diced tomatoes

2 teaspoons sugar

½ teaspoon dried basil leaves

¼ teaspoon crushed red pepper flakes

½ teaspoon salt

¼ teaspoon ground black pepper

½ cup Kitchen Basics chicken stock

1 (15-ounce) can tomato sauce

4 to 5 tablespoons tomato paste

½ cup water

1. Pour olive oil in a 6-quart saucepan and sauté onions and garlic about 2 to 3 minutes or until golden in color. Add tomatoes, sugar, basil leaves, red pepper flakes, salt, and pepper. Add the chicken stock and allow the spices and tomatoes to simmer together about 5 to 6 minutes.

2. Add the tomato sauce and paste, stirring well to break up the paste. Add the water, and a little more if needed for a smooth consistency. Let the sauce simmer on low heat about 8 minutes. Makes 4 cups.

Time: 10 Minutes

PEPPERMINT SAUCE

Note: *My father would grow peppermint every summer, and when he would barbecue meat, he would slather this sauce over the meat using peppermint sprigs. It was so good over beef, chicken, and even fish.*

¼ cup fresh peppermint leaves, packed

1 large clove garlic, chopped

1 large fresh tomato, cored, peeled and chopped fine, about 1 cup
   or ½ cup diced tomatoes, juice included

¼ cup extra virgin olive oil

2 tablespoons water

½ teaspoon lemon juice

½ teaspoon coarse sea salt

Place peppermint and chopped garlic in a wooden bowl and pound with a wooden pestle until smashed together, about 1 minute. Remove to a larger bowl and add the chopped tomato, olive oil, water, lemon juice and salt. Stir together until well blended. Makes 1 cup sauce.

Time: 5 Minutes

GARLIC BUTTER SAUCE

Note: *This sauce is perfect for your shrimp scampi, baked fish, and even over some vegetables dishes.*

½ cup sweet cream butter

2 teaspoons garlic, minced

2 teaspoons fresh squeezed lemon juice

1 tablespoon parsley, chopped fine

Coarse sea salt

Ground black pepper

Place butter in a small skillet and add garlic. Sauté garlic over low heat until lightly golden, about 30 seconds. Add the fresh lemon juice, parsley, salt and pepper to taste. Makes ½ cup.

Time: 10 Minutes

BASIL PESTO

Note: *There is nothing like fresh basil pesto to serve over your favorite pasta, pizza, bruschetta, or even as a dip with toasted pita wedges. Pesto sauce can also be frozen, but do not add the cheese until thawed, as cheese does not freeze well. Walnuts can also be used in place of pine nuts.*

2 cups fresh basil leaves

2 tablespoons pignoli (pine nuts) or walnuts

3 to 4 cloves garlic, chopped

1 cup extra virgin olive oil

¼ teaspoon coarse sea salt

Coarse ground black pepper

½ cup freshly grated Parmesan cheese

1. Wash basil leaves, pat dry and remove from stem. Measure out 2 cups basil leaves. Lightly toast pine nuts in a dry skillet over medium heat, stirring constantly for about 2 minutes. Place basil, toasted pine nuts, garlic, and ½ cup olive oil in a blender or food processor. Blend together using pulse speed just until blended, about 6 seconds. Add remaining ½ cup olive oil, salt and pepper, and pulse about 5 seconds longer. Sauce will be a puree consistency .

2. Pour pesto into a medium bowl. Add the cheese and whip together with a fork. Use immediately, or keep refrigerated in a jar with lid for up to one week. Makes 1½ cups pesto.

Chicken Parmigiana over Linguine
on page 186

MEAT, CHICKEN,
&FISH DISHES

Serving the Grand Entrée

Italian entrées are the part of the dish that makes the whole meal a star. It is the one thing that determines what we order when we go out to our favorite restaurant. We don't even care what comes with it, we just want to sink our teeth into that coveted dish. My mouth starts salivating just hearing the waiter suggest Chicken Piccata, or the Garlic Crusted Roast, complete with Italian Roasted Potatoes.

Maybe it's fish we are craving, and we know just where to go to get our favorite, Parmesan Crusted Cod, or the ever popular Shrimp Scampi. Whatever your favorite entrée, I do hope you will find it in this section. I have also included holiday entrées, such as the Roast Turkey with Italian Sausage Dressing, which my mother made every Thanksgiving. For Easter you may want to try the most wonderful Roast Leg of Lamb with Peppermint Sauce.

Cooking is one way our creative side expresses itself. So have fun making these wonderful entrées, and these recipes will soon become your own.

Tips for Entrées:

1. Serve the entrée in an attractive way, with vegetable or potato taking second place. Do not crowd the entrée.

2. Garnish the plate with a sprig of parsley, mint, rosemary, or curly kale. These garnishes give the meal a pleasant appeal.

3. Keep portions small enough, so your guest can have the option of having seconds. Piling too much on the plate overpowers the entrée.

4. If the entrée is one dish such as Chicken Cacciatore, or Chicken Parmigiana over Linguine, keep the side dishes minimal, such as one small vegetable and or salad.

5. Have flowers on the table, preferably fresh. This will tell everyone that your dinner is special and above all that your guests are special.

6. If you are going to make a special dinner for your guests, consider cloth napkins. They dress up the table, and a nice napkin holder tops off the place setting.

7. Again, if the dinner is for entertaining guests, complement the good food with a beautiful table. Don't just look at the china in the breakfront, get it out and proudly use it!

Garlic Crusted Roast
on page 168

Time: 20 Minutes

PEPPER CRUSTED FILET MIGNON WITH GARLIC BUTTER SAUCE

Note: *These little filets are so tasty and are complimented by a savory garlic butter sauce. Serve with Spaghetti alla Carbonara for a special occasion dinner!*

4 (5-ounce) bacon-wrapped filet mignon

Stonemill steak seasoning or favorite steak seasoning

Olive oil

2 tablespoons butter

2 large cloves garlic, chopped fine

1 tablespoon fresh curly parsley, chopped fine

½ cup heavy whipping cream

2 to 3 tablespoons Parmesan cheese

¼ teaspoon freshly ground black pepper

Parsley sprigs

1. Sprinkle filets on both sides with the steak seasoning. Pour olive oil in large skillet and over medium-high heat, sear filets for 6 to 8 minutes on each side for a medium rare to pink center; cook longer for desired doneness. Use meat thermometer pierced into each filet to reach 160 degrees for pink center. Turn filets once or twice to prevent burning. Remove to meat platter when filets are cooked to your liking.

2. Make the garlic/butter sauce by placing butter in a medium saucepan. Melt butter and add the garlic and parsley; heat to a sizzle, no more than 15 seconds. Add the cream and simmer until cream is very warm. Add the cheese and stir until sauce begins to thicken; add pepper and stir. Place about a tablespoon sauce over each steak and garnish with parsley sprigs. Serves 4.

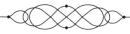
Time: 20 Minutes

SPIEDINI (STUFFED MEAT ROLLS)

Note: *I can't describe how delicious these little stuffed meat rolls are.*
You will just have to experience it for yourself. Serve with peppermint sauce for a delicious treat.

1 recipe **Peppermint Sauce** on page 161

1 (3-pound) top round roast, sliced in very thin steaks,
   or 12 thin breakfast steaks

Lawry's coarse garlic salt with parsley added

½ cup olive oil

1 cup plain bread crumbs

1 cup Parmesan cheese

3 cloves garlic, chopped thin

¼ cup fresh curly parsley, chopped

1 teaspoon coarse sea salt

½ teaspoon ground black pepper

12 slices Genoa salami

12 slices provolone cheese, halved

Olive oil

1. Preheat grill or oven to 350 degrees. Prepare pepper-mint sauce as directed; set aside. Sprinkle steaks lightly with garlic salt. Pour olive oil in shallow plate and dip steaks in olive oil on both sides; leave steaks in oil while making the breading.

2. Make the breading by placing the bread crumbs, cheese, garlic, parsley, salt, and pepper in a shallow plate; mix together well. Coat the oiled steaks in the bread crumb mixture on both sides. Working with one steak at a time, place one piece of salami and the two halves of the provolone over the steak. Starting at one end, roll the steak up tight, jelly-roll style, while tucking in the cheese. Secure rolls with sturdy toothpicks, and place seam side down on grill, or on large oiled baking sheet. If grilling spiedini, spray grill with cooking spray and grill rolls for 4 to 5 minutes on each side. If baking rolls, place on large baking sheet and bake for 20 minutes. Drizzle a little olive oil over the spiedini before cooking. Transfer spiedini to a large platter and serve with the peppermint sauce. Serves 12.

Time: 3 Hours

GARLIC CRUSTED ROAST

Note: *This roast is so good, you will want to make it again and again. It goes perfectly with the pan dripping gravy and the wonderful **Italian Roasted Potatoes** found on page 100.*

1 (4 to 5 pound) boneless rump roast

2 cloves garlic

¼ cup extra virgin olive oil

1 tablespoon coarse sea salt

1 teaspoon coarse ground black pepper

1 teaspoon dried oregano

½ teaspoon dried basil

3 cloves garlic, chopped fine

½ to 1 cup water

2 beef bouillon cubes

2 tablespoons flour

1 cup water

1. Preheat oven to 350 degrees. Make 6 deep slits all over the roast. Cut each of the two cloves of garlic into 3 length-wise cuts. Embed the cuts of garlic into the deep slits.

2. Pour olive oil into a small bowl. Add the salt, pepper, oregano, basil, and the chopped garlic. Make a rub of the garlic, spices, and olive oil, and rub the entire roast until evenly coated.

3. Place the roast on a rack in a shallow roasting pan and add the water to the bottom of the pan. Bake uncovered for 1½ to 2¼ hours for desired doneness. Insert meat thermometer into center of roast to read 145 degrees for a medium-rare roast and 160 degrees for a medium cooked roast (pink in the middle). Keep roasting the meat for well done, 170 degrees. Remove roast from oven and let stand for 10 to 15 minutes before slicing.

4. Pour the pan drippings in a small saucepan and add the beef bouillon cubes and bring to simmer. Add the flour to 1 cup cool water and stir in well to make it smooth and lump-free. Add the flour mixture to the pan drippings and over medium heat, stir until the gravy is thick and bubbly. Serve the gravy with the sliced roast, and **Italian Roasted Potatoes**. Serves 12.

Rosalie Serving Best Loved Italian

Time: 15 Minutes

GRILLED MODIGA STRIP STEAKS

Note: *My father, Bill Fiorino, would grill these steaks outside during the summer months. The smell would permeate the neighborhood, and everyone knew these scrumptious steaks were on the grill.*

1 recipe **Peppermint Sauce** on page 159

4 strip sirloin steaks

Lawry's coarse ground garlic salt with parsley added

½ cup extra virgin olive oil

1 cup plain bread crumbs

½ cup grated Parmesan cheese

3 cloves garlic, chopped

¼ cup fresh curly parsley, chopped

1 teaspoon coarse sea salt

¼ teaspoon ground black pepper

1. Rinse steaks in cool water. Pat dry and sprinkle with garlic salt on both sides. Pour olive oil in a large shallow dish and coat steaks on both sides. Leave steaks in oil and set aside.

2. Mix bread crumbs, cheese, garlic, parsley, salt, and pepper. Place the crumbs in a large shallow dish. Dip the oil-coated steaks in bread crumb mixture on both sides. Spray grill with cooking spray, and place on hot grill. Grill the steaks about 2 to 3 minutes on each side. Return steaks to large meat platter. Serve with peppermint sauce. Serves 4.

Sammy

Bailey

My Funny Dad
An Ode to Father's Day

Thinking about Father's Day and my dad makes me want to laugh. As some of you may know, my dad William Fiorino was 100% Italian, an immigrant from Rome, Italy. He was really a character to say the least and growing up with him was at times a cringing experience. He use to embarrass me so many times as a teenager because I never knew what he would say. For instance, when someone asked if he came from Italy as a child, he would reply, "Oh, yes, and actually I was conceived on the boat." Of course this was entirely possible, seeing that it took some 40 days to travel from Rome, Italy, to Ellis Island, and I'm sure they suffered their share of boredom.

He was very strict with me as a teenager growing up, and I can remember that he finally let me date Bill when I was 17 years old. When Bill came to the door to pick me up, my dad said, "Come on in, young man . . . I have a few words to say." It was usually a 15-minute lecture about curfew and safety, and treating his daughter with respect. He wished us a good time, noting that he had no problem calling on his Mafia friends if his daughter did not show up!

He was always very outgoing and boldness was his gift. For instance, my husband Bill and I pastored a small country church in Troy, Missouri for many years. One evening during the prayer service, we heard my dad whistle. He actually whistled pretty loud, then he said, "Jesus, you are so beautiful!" There happened to be two rows of youth sitting right in front of my dad, and when they heard Grandpa Fiorino whistling, they began to double over with laughter. That was only one of the many "church experiences" with Brother Fiorino. He really did love going to church, and especially kissing all the elderly ladies. When my mom would call him on it, he would just say, "I am spreading the love around, and besides, the widows have nothing to look forward to." I must say they did line up every Sunday. Mom would throw up her hands and say, "I give up."

He was a butcher for many years and worked as head manager for the National Food Stores. He would always arrive at his store two hours early and made sure his meat cases were all in order and cleaned. People would line up to buy his homemade Italian sausage, and of course hear him tell his jokes. A lady asked him one day if he had any fresh fish. He told her he would check, and brought a large catfish from the back of the store. He would flop the fish around to make it look like it was alive and then cut off its head. She was so satisfied; she never knew about Dad's trick. His customers could always count on him.

To say that he was proud of his wife and children was an understatement. He would pound his chest, and with tears in his eyes he would say, "I have the best children in the world." He did get frustrated with my mom because she was always two hours late, and he was always two hours early. Sometimes when they would go out, he would blow his car horn in the driveway several times for her to appear. The neighbors always enjoyed the show.

But my dad was truly a one-of-a-kind, jolly person. He was big-hearted and kind to everyone, and always had a positive word to say. When people were down, he would say, "Hey, you are in the best country in the world—America!" He would remind us all that our freedom was worth all the gold in the world, and that we should never take it for granted. I must say he was a good dad and I never doubted his love for me. He truly was My Funny Dad!

Happy Father's Day

Rosalie

Excerpts from Rosalie's monthly newsletter that you can sign up to receive at www.rosalieserving.com

Time: 15 Minutes

ITALIAN HAMBURGERS/MEATBALLS

Note: *These juicy hamburgers are wonderful and full of Italian flavor. You will use this recipe in so many ways, in your marinara sauce; for a quick pasta sauce, and even on pizzas and bruschetta. Also makes great Italian Hamburger sandwiches!*

1½ pounds ground chuck

3 cloves garlic, chopped

⅓ cup plain bread crumbs

⅓ cup Parmesan cheese

¼ cup fresh curly parsley, chopped

3 eggs

½ teaspoon fennel seeds

1 teaspoon salt

¼ teaspoon ground black pepper

Olive oil

1 loaf Italian sliced bread, optional

In large bowl, mix together the ground chuck, garlic, bread crumbs, cheese, parsley, eggs, fennel seeds, salt, and pepper. Make into patties, or meatballs. Fry in olive oil over medium heat 4 to 5 minutes on each side. Makes 6 large patties or 12 meatballs.

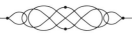

Time: 1 Hour 20 Minutes

ROSALIE'S ITALIAN MEATLOAF

Note: *This meatloaf is absolutely delicious with lots of sauce to garnish your garlic mashed potatoes . . . yum!*

1 recipe **Rosalie's Marinara Sauce** on page 160

2 pounds lean ground beef

1 pound lean ground pork

1 cup plain bread crumbs

½ cup Pecorino Romano grated cheese

2 eggs

½ cup whole tomatoes, chopped fine with juice included

1 (8-ounce) can tomato sauce

½ cup onion, chopped fine

⅓ cup fresh curly parsley, chopped

1 teaspoon crushed red pepper flakes

1 tablespoon salt

1 teaspoon coarse ground black pepper

Olive oil

1. Preheat oven to 375 degrees. Prepare marinara sauce as directed; set aside. In large mixing bowl, mix the ground beef and ground pork with clean hands. Add the bread crumbs, cheese, eggs, tomatoes, tomato sauce, onion, parsley, crushed red pepper flakes, salt, and pepper. Mix together until well combined, crushing the tomatoes into the meat. Place the meat into a well-oiled large baking pan and shape into one large loaf, evenly distributing the meat.

2. Bake the meatloaf for 30 minutes uncovered, then remove from oven. Spread 1 cup of the marinara sauce over the meat and return to oven uncovered for another 30 to 40 minutes, or until a meat thermometer inserted into the meat registers 160 degrees. Remove from pan and place on a large platter. Let meatloaf rest for 5 to 10 minutes before slicing. Pass the marinara sauce at the table for spooning over meatloaf. Serves 10.

Time: 1 Hour 30 Minutes

ITALIAN HOMEMADE SALSICCIA

Note: *This recipe is in memory of my father, Bill Fiorino, who made this wonderful homemade sausage for the enjoyment of our family and friends. If you do not have a meat grinder or attachments, you can still make this sausage in bulk form and make it into sausage patties.*

1 meat grinder or funnel attachment

4 pounds ground pork

2 pounds ground beef

1 cup Pecorino Romano cheese, grated

1 (15-ounce) can whole tomatoes, chopped fine and juice included

2 tablespoons fennel seeds

2 teaspoons crushed red pepper flakes

2 tablespoons salt

1 teaspoon coarse ground black pepper

25 feet pork casing

1. Place ground pork and beef in a large bowl; using clean hands, mix the two meats together well. Add the cheese, tomatoes, fennel seeds, red pepper flakes, salt, and pepper. Mix the meat and seasonings together well. Cover the bowl with plastic wrap and leave in refrigerator for 3 to 4 hours to rest and combine flavors.

2. Clean casing by pushing about 1 inch of one end of the casing over the spout of faucet in your sink, making sure the rest of the casing remains in the sink. Turn on water and gently wash out casing to remove any preserving salts or residue. Remove casing from spout. When meat is ready to stuff, use the stuffing attachment on meat grinder to make sausage links. Twist the sausage into 3½-inch links.

3. If making patties, roll meat into rolls with your hands and then flatten. Place patties on wax paper and then seal in clear wrap. Store in plastic freezer bag in freezer. Makes 6 pounds of sausage.

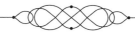

Time: 1½ Hours

ITALIAN BEEF STEW

Note: *My mother would make this wonderful stew, adding a can of diced tomatoes along with the good vegetables to give it an Italian touch.*

1 pound lean stew meat

Lawry's coarse garlic salt with parsley added

½ cup all-purpose flour

½ teaspoon salt

½ teaspoon pepper

⅓ cup mild olive oil

4 cups Kitchen Basics low-sodium beef stock

2 cups water

2 medium onions, small quartered

3 to 4 large carrots, cut into 1-inch pieces

4 stalks celery, cut into 1-inch pieces

2 medium russet potatoes, unpeeled and small quartered

½ pound green beans, fresh or frozen, chopped small

1 cup frozen peas

1 (15-ounce) can diced tomatoes

1 envelope Lipton Recipe Secrets Beefy Onion Soup Mix

2 tablespoons flour

⅓ cup cool water

Salt and pepper

1. Rinse meat under cool water in drainer; pat dry and sprinkle liberally with garlic salt. In medium bowl, combine the flour, salt, and pepper. Dredge meat in seasoned flour and brown on both sides in hot oil in large electric skillet, or large saucepan, until meat is no longer pink, about 8 to 10 minutes.

2. Add beef stock and water to pan and let liquid come to a boil. Simmer gently for about 10 minutes.

3. Next, add onions, carrots, celery, potatoes, green beans, peas and tomatoes. Stir well and place lid on pan; simmer for 1 hour. Stir stew occasionally to prevent vegetables from sticking.

4. Remove lid and add soup mix and stir well. Place flour in measuring cup and add water; stir to make thin paste. Add flour mixture to stew and stir to thicken, keeping stew on gentle simmer. If thicker gravy is desired, make another flour/water mixture and add to stew. Taste for flavor and add additional salt and pepper if desired. Serve with crusty bread or roll. Serves 6 to 8.

Time: 1 Hour, 15 Minutes

ITALIAN STUFFED BELL PEPPERS

Note: *These peppers are awesome with plenty of sauce for everyone. The colors over the rice will make the dish very appealing.*

6 medium bell peppers (multi-colored)

1 pound ground chuck

¼ cup grated Parmesan cheese

¼ cup plain bread crumbs

2 cloves garlic, chopped

2 tablespoons fresh curly parsley, chopped

2 eggs

1 teaspoon salt

¼ teaspoon ground black pepper

¼ cup olive oil, divided

½ cup celery, chopped small

⅓ cup onion, chopped small

1 (15-ounce) can diced tomatoes, juice included

1 teaspoon sugar

½ teaspoon dried basil leaves

½ teaspoon salt

¼ teaspoon ground black pepper

1 (15-ounce) can tomato sauce

1 cup shredded Parmesan cheese

1 cup shredded mozzarella cheese

Curley parsley, chopped

3 cups cooked rice (optional)

1. Preheat oven to 350 degrees. Cut tops off each pepper to ¼-inch down. Remove inside seeds and ribs. Wash the peppers in cool water; pat dry and set aside.

2. In large bowl, mix the ground chuck, cheese, bread crumbs, garlic, parsley, eggs, salt, and pepper until well combined. Divide the meat among the peppers; set aside.

3. Make the sauce by pouring the olive oil in a large skillet. Add the celery and the onion and sauté until translucent, 4 to 5 minutes. Add the tomatoes, sugar, basil, salt, and pepper; simmer 5 minutes. Add tomato sauce and simmer another 5 minutes. Remove the sauce from heat and top each pepper with sauce and place in a 9x13-inch baking pan. Cover with foil and bake 30 minutes. Remove pan from oven; remove foil. Divide the cheeses over the peppers and place back in oven for 5 minutes to melt cheese. Garnish peppers with chopped parsley. Serve peppers with additional sauce.

4. If using rice, boil rice to make 3 cups, and arrange peppers over rice and sauce. Serves 8.

BRACIOLE
(STUFFED ROLLED STEAK)

Note: *This is an Italian classic usually meant for a Sunday afternoon meal or for a special occasion. A large slice of meat, usually a flank steak, is topped with an Italian stuffing and then rolled. It is then baked or simmered in a large pot of marinara or meat sauce and becomes very tender. It can be served alone with a favorite side dish or with pasta. My mother would actually cook the braciole in her Sunday sauce, excluding all other meat except her meatballs. She would boil up a couple pounds of pasta, and serve it with the sliced braciole. What a treat!*

1 recipe **Rosalie's Meat Sauce** on page 158

1 beef flank steak, about 1½ pounds

1 tablespoons extra virgin olive oil

Lawry's coarse garlic salt with parsley added

½ cup Italian style bread crumbs

½ cup Parmesan cheese

2 cloves garlic, chopped fine

2 tablespoons fresh curly parsley, chopped

½ teaspoon salt

¼ teaspoon ground black pepper

1 tablespoon olive oil

½ pound sweet ground Italian sausage

1 cup shredded provolone

Strong toothpicks

Kitchen string

Olive oil

½ cup Kitchen Basics beef stock

1. Preheat oven to 350 degrees. Prepare marinara sauce as directed; set aside. Lay the flank steak on a large wooden cutting board and pound the steak with a wooden mallet to flatten to a ½-inch thickness. Rub the steak with the olive oil and sprinkle with the garlic salt.

2. Make the breading by placing bread crumbs, cheese, garlic, parsley, salt, and pepper into a bowl and add the tablespoon of olive oil to moisten the crumbs. Spread the crumbs over the steak.

3. Brown the sausage lightly in skillet and crumble; do not cook completely. Place the crumbled sausage over the bread crumbs. Lastly, spread the shredded provolone over the sausage. Roll the steak up jelly-roll style, trying to keep as much of the stuffing intact as possible. Secure with toothpicks temporarily. Tie the roll up with heavy kitchen string in four places to secure, then remove toothpicks. Pour olive oil in the bottom of a very large skillet and sear the rolled steak on all sides, about 8 minutes. At the end of searing, add the beef stock to loosen the steak bits and preserve flavor.

4. Place the stuffed steak and drippings into a large Dutch oven, and cook on stove top, or place braciole in a deep baking pan to be baked in the oven. Add the marinara sauce over the steak and cook on stove top over low heat for 1½ hours, or until fork tender. If baking braciole, place it in a deep baking pan with the marinara and cover with foil or lid for 1 ½ hours. Check on the braciole occasionally to avoid sticking to bottom of pan.

5. When cooking is completed, remove the braciole to a large flat platter surrounded with the marinara sauce. Slice into ½-inch slices and serve with Italian salad and vegetable, or with your favorite pasta. Serves 8 to 10.

 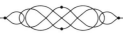

Time: 20 Minutes

ITALIAN BREADED PORK CHOPS

Note: *These chops are so delicious, it is hard to describe. They are easy and quick to make and your family will love the tender melt-in-your- mouth meat.*

4 to 6 (bone-in) pork chops

Lawry's coarse garlic salt
with parsley added

2 eggs, beaten

1 cup plain bread crumbs

⅓ cup grated Parmesan cheese

2 cloves garlic, chopped

¼ cup fresh curly parsley, chopped

1 teaspoon salt,

¼ teaspoon ground black pepper

Olive oil

Peppermint sprigs

1. Rinse chops under cool water, pat dry. Sprinkle the chops lightly with the garlic salt; set aside. Place the beaten eggs in a shallow pie plate. Make the breading by combining the bread crumbs, cheese, garlic, parsley, salt, and pepper. Place the bread crumb mixture in another shallow pie plate. Dip the chops in the egg on both sides, and then into the bread crumb mixture on both sides.

2. Pour olive oil in the bottom of a large skillet, and fry the chops in medium hot oil about 3 to 4 minutes on each side. Lower the heat and put the lid on the pan. Let the chops steam up, about another 8 to 10 minutes. Remove the breaded chops to a large meat platter. Garnish with peppermint sprigs. Makes 4 to 6 servings.

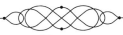

Time: 2 Hours, 30 Minutes

ROAST PORK LOIN
WITH FENNEL AND GARLIC

Note: *The garlic and fennel embedded into the roast give the meat a distinct flavor, not too heavy, but notable.*
Serve with your favorite side dishes.

1 (3-pound) pork roast

2 large cloves garlic

1 teaspoon fennel seed

Lawry's coarse garlic salt with
   parsley added

½ teaspoon ground black pepper

1 teaspoon ground fennel

Flour

¼ cup olive oil

1 large onion, small quartered

2 stalks celery, chopped medium

10 baby carrots

1 (8-ounce) package white button
   mushrooms, stems removed and
   left whole

1 teaspoon salt

¼ teaspoon ground black pepper

2 cups Kitchen Basics beef stock

2 tablespoons flour

½ cup water

1. Preheat oven to 350 degrees. Rinse roast under cool water; pat dry. Slice garlic into six slivers. Insert six deep slits into the roast with small sharp knife in various places. Embed the slivers of garlic into the six slits. Make four additional deep slits, and place ¼ teaspoon fennel seed in each slit. Sprinkle the entire roast with the garlic salt and pepper. Rub the entire top of roast with the ground fennel. Next, coat the entire roast with flour and sear roast in hot oil in a large skillet on all sides, about 8 to 10 minutes. Remove roast and place into a large baking pan.

2. Place the onion, celery, carrots, and mushrooms all around the roast. Sprinkle salt and pepper on the vegetables. Add the beef stock and roast uncovered in the oven for about 1 hour. Cover the roast with lid or foil and continue to bake another 30 minutes. Pork is done when thermometer placed in thick part of roast reads 175 degrees.

3. Transfer roast to large meat platter. Place vegetables around the roast and place drippings in medium saucepan. Add the flour to the cool water and stir until smooth and lump-free. Bring the pan drippings to a gentle boil and stir in the flour mixture quickly. Continue to stir until the gravy is thick and bubbly. Serve gravy with roast and with favorite potato side dish. Serves 6 to 8.

VEAL PARMIGIANA

Note: *This dish is a classic Italian-American dish and is still served in many Italian restaurants. Veal can be very expensive, and if unable to find, pork cutlets can be substituted.*

1 recipe **Rosalie's Marinara Sauce**
   on page 160

8 veal cutlets, sliced thin

Lawry's coarse garlic salt
   with parsley added

2 eggs, beaten

1 cup plain bread crumbs

⅓ cup grated Parmesan cheese

2 cloves garlic, chopped

¼ cup fresh curly parsley, chopped

1 teaspoon salt

¼ teaspoon ground black pepper

Olive oil

1 cup Parmesan cheese

8 slices provolone cheese

Peppermint or basil sprigs

1. Preheat oven to 400 degrees. Prepare the marinara sauce according to directions; set aside. Rinse cutlets in cool water; pat dry. Lightly sprinkle the cutlets with the garlic salt; set aside. Beat the eggs and place in a shallow pie plate; set aside.

2. Make the breading by combining the bread crumbs, cheese, garlic, parsley, salt, and pepper. Mix together well and place in another shallow pie plate. Dip the cutlets in the egg, and then coat on both sides in the bread crumb mixture. Pour olive oil to cover bottom of large skillet. Over medium heat, fry the breaded cutlets about 2 to 3 minutes on each side.

3. Spray bottom of a 13x9-inch baking pan with cooking spray. Arrange the cutlets on bottom of pan; cutlets can overlap somewhat. Pour 2 cups of the prepared marinara sauce over the cutlets. Sprinkle the Parmesan cheese over the marinara. Place 1 slice of the provolone over each cutlet. Bake uncovered 8 to 10 minutes to melt cheeses. Sauce should be bubbly. Transfer cutlets to serving dish and garnish with peppermint sprigs. Serve with favorite pasta if desired. Serve remaining marinara at the table if desired. Serves 8.

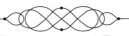
Time: 2 Hours

OSSO BUCO (BRAISED VEAL SHANKS)

Note: *Osso buco means "bone with hole" pertaining to the bone marrow on the shank. Italians eat this bone marrow as a delicacy. It is a very rich and savory dish. Veal shanks can be pricey, so reserve the dish for special guests.*

4 veal shanks, 2 inches thick, about 1 pound each

Lawry's coarse garlic salt with parsley added

Ground black pepper

½ cup flour

3 to 4 tablespoons olive oil

½ cup water

¼ cup olive oil

1 medium onion, chopped

3 cloves garlic, chopped fine

2 stalks celery with leaves, chopped ½-inch slices

1 large carrot, chopped small

1 teaspoon coarse sea salt

2 teaspoons tomato paste

4 cups Kitchen Basics chicken stock

1 sprig fresh thyme or dried thyme

1 bay leaf

¼ cup fresh Italian flat-leaf parsley, chopped

Gremolata Sauce

1 tablespoon lemon zest

2 tablespoons fresh Italian flat-leaf parsley, chopped fine

1 small clove garlic, minced

1. Preheat oven to 375 degrees. Rinse shanks in cool water; pat dry. Sprinkle shanks on all sides with the garlic salt and pepper and roll the shanks in the flour to coat. In large skillet, heat the oil and brown the shanks on all sides, 8 to 10 minutes. The meat should have a crusty brown coating. Transfer the shanks to a large roasting pan. Deglaze the searing pan with ½ cup water. Heat the water to gather the meat bits and juice and pour over the meat.

2. In clean fry pan, pour the olive oil and sauté the onion, garlic, celery, and carrot. Sprinkle the vegetables with salt and pepper while frying for about 6 minutes. Add the tomato paste and work into the vegetables. Add the vegetables to the roaster with the chicken stock, fresh thyme, bay leaf, and parsley.

3. Cover the pan with lid or aluminum foil and braise in the oven for about 1 ½ hours. Turn the veal shanks over once or twice during cooking. The meat should be fork-tender. Transfer to a large meat platter and place the vegetables all around the meat. Make the gremolata sauce by combining the lemon zest, parsley, and garlic. Toss together and serve over the meat, if desired. Serves 4.

Time: 3 Hours

ROAST LEG OF LAMB
WITH PEPPERMINT SAUCE

Note: *This beautiful entrée is the ideal thing to serve on Easter Sunday, and a great alternative for the traditional ham. Even if you don't like lamb, you may just want to try this.*

1 recipe **Peppermint Sauce** on page 161

1 recipe **Italian Roasted Vegetables** on page 91

1 leg of lamb

2 cloves garlic

¼ cup fresh lemon juice

2 tablespoons extra virgin olive oil

1 tablespoon salt

2 teaspoons coarse ground black pepper

3 tablespoons fresh rosemary leaves, chopped fine

2 tablespoons fresh peppermint, chopped fine

1 tablespoon dried thyme

6 cloves garlic, minced

¼ cup fresh lemon juice

¼ cup extra virgin olive oil

2 tablespoons butter, melted

1. Preheat oven to 400 degrees. Prepare peppermint sauce according to directions; set aside. Prepare Italian roasted vegetables, if desired, while baking roast. Cut 2 cloves of garlic into six slices; make slits in roast and insert a garlic sliver in each.

2. In small bowl, pour lemon juice, olive oil, salt, black pepper, rosemary, peppermint, thyme, and garlic. Stir well to make a rub, and coat the entire roast with the rub. Place the lamb, fat side up, on a rack in a large roasting pan. Insert meat thermometer, making sure it does not touch fat or bone. Roast the lamb for 30 minutes, then reduce heat to 325 degrees. Continue to cook for about another 1½ hours. For medium rare, thermometer should read 145-150 degrees. For a more pink meat, cook lamb to 160 degrees.

3. Make basting sauce by placing lemon juice, olive oil and butter in a bowl. Baste roast two to three times during roasting. Remove from oven when roast is cooked to your liking, and place on large meat platter. Surround roast with roasted vegetables. Serve with Peppermint Sauce and Italian Roasted Vegetables. Serves 10.

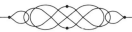
Time: 20 Minutes

ITALIAN CRUSTED CHICKEN

Note: *This is my version of fried chicken. It is crusted on the outside, and juicy on the inside. It is great served with **Classic Fettuccine Alfredo** on page 150.*

4 skinless chicken breasts, medium sliced

Lawry's coarse garlic salt with parsley added

1 cup flour

3 tablespoons grated Parmesan cheese

¼ teaspoon paprika

1 teaspoon salt

½ teaspoon ground black pepper

2 eggs, beaten

Olive oil

Parsley sprigs

1. Rinse chicken breasts in cool water; pat dry. Remove any fat or hard gristle from breasts. Cut each breasts in half for smaller portions. Sprinkle chicken on both sides with the garlic salt.

2. Combine the flour, cheese, paprika, salt, and pepper in a shallow bowl. Dip the chicken in the beaten eggs and coat chicken on both sides with the flour mixture. Pour olive oil in a large skillet, enough to cover bottom of pan. Fry the chicken over medium heat 4 to 5 minutes on each side. Place lid on pan and steam the chicken about another 6 to 8 minutes, or until tender. Transfer to large platter and garnish with parsley sprigs. Serves 4 to 6.

Jennifer and Scott Harpole

Time: 20 Minutes

PAN-FRIED BREADED CHICKEN TENDERLOINS

Note: *This dish is a favorite of my family, and even the grandchildren can make these yummy cutlets.*

1 pound chicken tenderloins

Lawry's coarse garlic salt with parsley added

2 large eggs

½ cup Progresso Italian bread crumbs

½ cup grated Parmesan cheese

2 cloves garlic, chopped fine

2 tablespoons fresh curly parsley, chopped fine

¼ teaspoon salt

¼ teaspoon ground black pepper

Olive oil

Parsley sprigs

1. Rinse chicken tenderloins in cool water; pat dry. Sprinkle the tenderloins with the garlic salt. Beat the eggs and place in a shallow pie plate; set aside.

2. Make the breading by combining the bread crumbs, cheese, garlic, parsley, salt, and pepper. Dip each tenderloin in the eggs, and then into the bread crumbs; coat each side well. Pour olive oil into large skillet, enough to cover bottom of pan. Fry the tenderloins over medium heat about 2 to 3 minutes on each side. Place lid on pan and steam the chicken about another 6 to 8 minutes, or until tender. Remove chicken to platter and serve warm. Garnish with parsley sprigs. Serves 4 to 6.

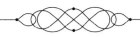
ITALIAN BREADED CHICKEN ROLLS

Note: *These warm chicken rolls will burst with flavor in your mouth.*
They were adopted from the Roman dish, Veal Saltimbocca, using chicken filets instead.

6 thin skinless chicken filets

Olive oil

Lawry's coarse garlic salt with parsley

2 eggs

½ cup Italian bread crumbs

½ cup grated Parmesan cheese

2 cloves garlic, chopped fine

2 tablespoons curly parsley, chopped

½ teaspoon salt

½ teaspoon ground black pepper

1 (10-ounce) package frozen spinach, thawed and drained

2 tablespoons olive oil

Salt and pepper

6 slices prosciutto

1 cup rope Provel cheese, divided or 3 slices provolone cheese, halved

Olive oil

1. Rinse chicken in cool water; pat dry. Filets should be about ⅛" thick. If too thick, pound the filets between waxed paper to flatten. Brush olive oil on both sides and sprinkle with garlic salt.

2. Beat the eggs until frothy. Mix bread crumbs, cheese, garlic, parsley, salt, and pepper; put the bread crumb mixture in a shallow plate. Dip the filets into the egg mixture and then into the bread crumbs on both sides. Set aside on cutting board.

3. Squeeze the thawed spinach to remove any excess water and place in small bowl. Add the olive oil with a little salt and pepper to flavor the spinach, mixing with fork to combine. Keep breaded filets on cutting board and place 1 slice of prosciutto over the chicken. Next, add about 1 tablespoon of the spinach. Lastly, add some of rope Provel, or half slice of the provolone. Roll each fillet up jelly-roll style; secure with a several strong toothpicks.

4. Pour olive oil into a large skillet to cover the bottom of pan. Fry the rolls over medium heat about 2 to 3 minutes on each side. Remove some of the toothpicks if they hinder turning the rolls. Fry until golden brown; remove to platter and garnish with parsley sprigs. Makes 6 rolls.

Time: 45 Minutes

CHICKEN PARMIGIANA
OVER LINGUINE

Note: *This dish is so easy and delicious, you will make it often. It is great with your favorite Italian salad and bread.*
See photo on page 163.

1 recipe **Rosalie's Marinara Sauce**
   on page 160

8 boneless chicken breasts,
   sliced medium

Lawry's garlic salt with parsley added

Olive oil

1 cup flour

⅓ cup grated Parmesan cheese

½ teaspoon salt

½ teaspoon ground black pepper

3 eggs, beaten

Olive oil

8 slices provolone cheese

1 to 1½ cups grated Parmesan cheese

1 pound linguine

1 tablespoon salt

Curly parsley, chopped fine
   or chopped chives

1.   Preheat oven to 350 degrees. Prepare marinara sauce as directed; set aside. Rinse chicken breasts in cool water; pat dry. If chicken breasts are thick, cut horizontally into medium slices. Sprinkle breasts with the garlic salt on both sides.

2.   Combine flour, cheese, salt, and pepper in shallow pie plate. Place beaten eggs in another shallow dish. Dip chicken breasts in eggs on both sides, and then into the flour mixture, coating well. In large saucepan, fry chicken in olive oil over medium heat 4 to 5 minutes on each side. Place lid on pan and turn heat to medium-low. Let the chicken steam for about 6 to 8 minutes. Transfer chicken to baking dish, and cover with 1½ cups marinara sauce. Top each breast with 1 slice provolone cheese. Sprinkle provolone with Parmesan cheese. Bake in oven uncovered 8 minutes to melt cheese.

3.   Boil linguine in an 8-quart pot of boiling water with salt added. Boil for 9 to 10 minutes according to package directions to al dente. Using a spaghetti spoon, lift the linguine right out of the water and into a large pasta bowl. Add the remaining marinara sauce and toss together well. Divide the linguine into 8 serving plates. Place 1 chicken parmigiana over the linguine. Sprinkle with more Parmesan cheese, if desired, and sprinkle with chopped parsley, or chopped chives. Serves 8.

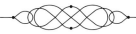

Time: 20 Minutes

CHICKEN PICCATA

Note: *This is a popular Italian chicken dish with a wonderful butter lemon sauce that gives it a rich and savory flavor. Your family will love this dish.*

4 skinless chicken breasts, medium sliced

Lawry's coarse garlic salt with parsley added

½ cup all-purpose flour

¼ cup extra virgin olive oil

3 tablespoons butter

½ cup Kitchen Basics chicken stock

⅓ cup freshly squeezed lemon juice

¼ cup capers, drained and rinsed

¼ cup Italian flat-leaf parsley, chopped

Coarse ground black pepper

1 tablespoon butter

1 teaspoon lemon juice

Peppermint sprigs

1. Rinse chicken in cool water; pat dry. Remove any fat or hard gristle from breasts. Sprinkle both sides with the garlic salt and dredge in flour.

2. Heat the oil and butter together in large skillet over medium heat and fry the chicken 4 to 5 minutes on each side until crusted and golden brown. Carefully remove the chicken using a flat server and place onto a large platter.

3. In same pan, add the chicken stock, lemon juice, capers, and fresh parsley. Scrape bottom of pan to loosen any chicken breading and whisk together over medium heat. Place the chicken breasts back into the pan and simmer with lid on for 6 to 8 minutes. Remove lid and sprinkle lightly with the coarse black pepper.

4. Transfer chicken back to platter carefully with a flat server, so as not to remove coating. Add the butter and lemon juice back to pan and heat together for 30 seconds; pour the hot sauce over chicken. Garnish platter with peppermint sprigs. Serves 4.

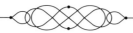
Time: 1 Hour, 15 Minutes

CHICKEN CACCIATORE

Note: *This dish is laden with sweet peppers, onion, and mushrooms complete with savory chicken. It is truly an Italian classic.*

12 ounces long curly pasta,
   or egg noodles

1 teaspoon salt

4 chicken thighs

2 chicken breasts, halved

Lawry's coarse garlic salt
   with parsley added

½ cup all-purpose flour

1 teaspoon salt

½ teaspoon ground black pepper

3 to 4 tablespoons olive oil

2 tablespoons butter

2 large red bell peppers, sliced medium

2 large green bell peppers,
   sliced medium

1 medium onion, small quartered

1 (8-ounce) carton mushrooms,
   thick-sliced, about 2 cups

5 to 6 cloves garlic, chopped fine

1½ teaspoons dried oregano

½ teaspoon crushed red pepper flakes

¾ cup Kitchen Basics chicken stock

1 (28-ounce) can diced tomatoes
   with juice

3 tablespoons capers, rinsed

½ cup reserved pasta water

2 tablespoons fresh curly parsley

Freshly ground black pepper

1.   Rinse chicken in cool water; pat dry. Remove fat and skin if desired; sprinkle the chicken lightly with the coarse garlic salt on both sides. Dredge in flour combined with salt and black pepper. In large skillet, or large electric skillet, add the olive oil and butter. Add the chicken pieces to the pan and sauté just until browned, about 6 to 7 minutes on each side. Remove chicken to platter; set aside.

2.   In same skillet, add the bell peppers, onion, and mushrooms. Sauté the vegetables over medium heat about 2 to 3 minutes to keep the vegetables crisp tender. Add the garlic, oregano, and red pepper flakes and continue to stir-fry another minute.

3.   Add the chicken stock, tomatoes, and capers. Return chicken over the vegetables. Put lid on skillet and bring to gentle simmer over low heat. Simmer the chicken and vegetables for 30 to 35 minutes without removing lid. Turn heat off after 35 minutes and keep lid on another 10 minutes while boiling pasta.

4.   Cook pasta according to package directions in an 8-quart pot of boiling water with salt added. Drain pasta, reserving ½ cup pasta water and place in large pasta platter. Place the vegetables and sauce over the pasta. Place the chicken over the vegetables. If pasta gets dry, add the reserved pasta water to refresh the dish. Sprinkle dish with parsley. Serves 6 to 8.

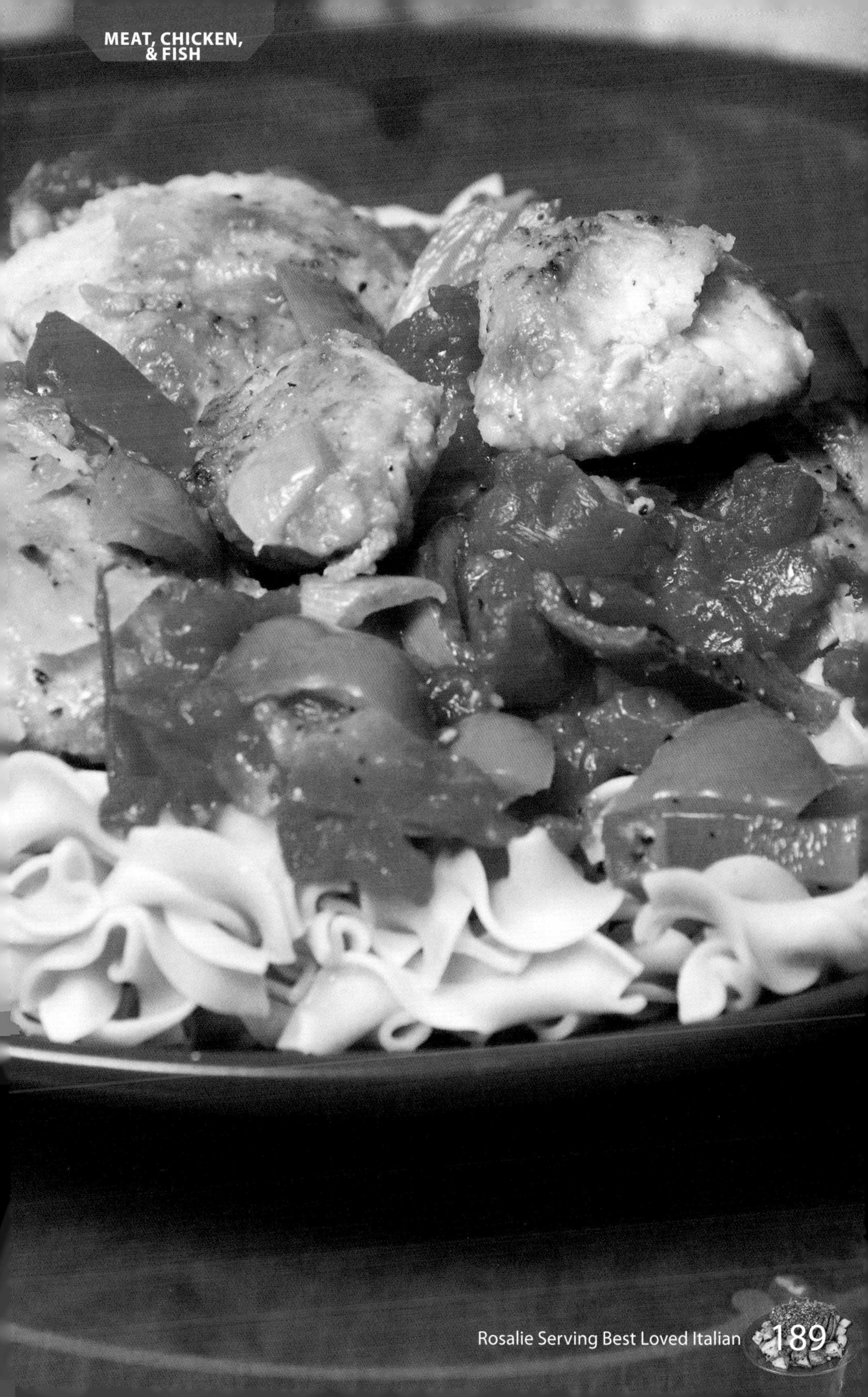

FOREVER & THANKSGIVING

When I think about the career that I have had as a registered nurse, it makes me so thankful to have had the luxury of witnessing the miraculous hand of God in the lives of so many. As it gets closer to the Thanksgiving holidays, I am blessed among women to have an intact family where everyone loves one another and holds the other dear. This is not true of every family, and one of those memories as a nurse proves this statement accurate.

It was a few years ago when I was taking care of a sweet lady who came into the hospital with a common illness. While taking care of her, as in so many cases, she told me the story of her two daughters. Sadly, she was divorced when they were sixteen, and eighteen-years-old. The sixteen-year-old daughter stayed with her, but the eighteen-year-old chose to go with her father. The father was very bitter and filled the older daughter daily with much disdain for her mother. Because the older daughter took up an offense for her father, she chose not to speak to her mother. My patient explained that she too became angry at the daughter, and as the years went by, neither would contact the other.

What seemed to be a routine diagnosis and treatment for this patient, with the usual expected outcome of healing, turned into a life-threatening situation. Within a few days, the patient became increasingly worse, in so much that all of her organs, one by one began shutting down. The doctor came to me and said, "I have spoken to her daughter and she wants to abide by her mother's wishes not to prolong life. Just make her comfortable; she will not live through the night."

Entering her room with despair hanging like a cloud, I found her crying. After giving her as much assurance as I could, I asked her if I could pray with her. She quickly said yes, and I asked God to come to her and give her peace. Shortly after, she became unresponsive with her daughter at the bedside. The following day, she was still with us, and the daughter asked if she could speak to me. "Should I call my sister?" she asked. "I don't even know if I have a number, but perhaps I could call someone who may." I immediately said, "Yes"; what could it hurt?

After many attempts, the younger daughter reached her sister. Miraculously, she was not far away and she told her sister, "I have been waiting for this phone call, and I so want to come." No one on the medical staff could believe the next few hours. The older daughter came and sat at her mother's side, talking to her and asking her to forgive the breach that had gone on so foolishly over the years. Was it the daughter's voice that woke her mother? Or was it the loving kindness of a miraculous God? The scene that etched in our hearts that day will never leave us. We saw two women crying, hugging, talking, and healing one another for the next few hours. Death came, but only after two sisters became reunited, and a mother and daughter were set free from the prison of bitterness.

The estranged sisters thanked all of us for the prayers and expressed great regret for the loss of the years. They stated that for the first time in many years they would enjoy the upcoming Thanksgiving holiday, sharing it with one another. Finally, they could have a *Forever Thanksgiving.*

Life is so short, and a root of bitterness can spring up overnight, defiling all it touches. The table will be set with wonderful food, but love and forgiveness will give it purpose. To love one another and make peace; this is the will of God for our lives.

Happy Thanksgiving

Rosalie

Excerpts from Rosalie's monthly newsletter that you can sign up to receive at www.rosalieserving.com

Time:3½ Hours

ROAST TURKEY WITH ITALIAN SAUSAGE DRESSING

Note: *Every Thanksgiving, my mother would make this turkey with the Italian sausage dressing, and for my brother, who had to have some pasta, she would still make her Sunday sauce.*

1 (12-14) pound turkey

1 apple, cored and quartered

1 medium onion, quartered

2 celery stalks, cut in thirds

2 to 3 tablespoons olive oil

Salt

Ground black pepper

1 cup water

½ cup butter

2½ cups celery, cut small

2 cups onion, cut small

½ teaspoon salt

¼ teaspoon ground black pepper

1 teaspoon dried sage

1½ teaspoon poultry seasoning

1 pound ground Italian sausage

3 eggs, beaten

2 cups Kitchen Basics chicken stock

½ cup turkey broth from drippings

Italian Sausage Dressing

1 loaf Italian bread, about 3 to 4 days old, cut up small, about 12 cups

1. Preheat oven to 350 degrees. Remove giblets and neck from turkey; discard or use for giblet gravy if desired. Rinse turkey with cold water; pat dry. If stuffing turkey, lightly stuff dressing into body cavities of turkey. If not, place the apple, onion, and celery stalks in large cavity. Close cavities with excess skin using skewers to hold skin in place. Tie ends of legs to tail with kitchen string.

2. Place turkey breast-side up in a large shallow roasting pan. Brush the skin with the olive oil, salt, and pepper the turkey liberally. Pour water into bottom of pan and baste turkey occasionally with the drippings during the baking time. Roast turkey according to package directions, or until the meat releases clear juices when pricked deeply with a fork. Meat thermometer should read 160 degrees. Turkey should roast 15 to 20 minutes per pound. If turkey starts to brown too much, cover loosely with aluminum foil.

3. Make the dressing by placing bread cubes into a large bowl; set aside. If bread is still too soft, place broken pieces on baking sheet and bake in oven for about 10 minutes until toasted. Place the butter in a large skillet and sauté the celery and onion until translucent, about 5 to 6 minutes. Add the salt, pepper, sage, and poultry seasoning, and let simmer another minute. Remove the celery/onion mixture to the bowl with the bread and toss together. In another skillet, brown the sausage until no longer pink, about 6 to 7 minutes. Drain grease and add to the bread mixture in the bowl; stir together. Beat the eggs in a medium bowl until lemon colored and add the chicken stock; stir together well. Pour the egg mixture over the bread and with clean hands, mix together well. If stuffing turkey, use both cavities and pack with dressing. If baking in oven, spray a 13x9-inch baking pan

with cooking spray and place the dressing into the pan. Bake covered for 45 minutes. Uncover and pour about ½ cup turkey drippings or chicken stock over top and continue to bake another 8 to 10 minutes uncovered for a golden crust.

4. Remove turkey to large platter and garnish with kale, red and green apples, and cranberries. Serves 12.

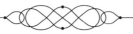

Time: 10 Minutes

TURKEY GRAVY

Note: *Rich turkey gravy is so easy to make, and this recipe uses just the right steps for perfect gravy every time.*

4 cups broth from turkey drippings
    or Kitchen Basics chicken stock

⅔ cup cool water

½ cup flour

Salt and pepper

Pour turkey drippings into a heavy 4-quart saucepan. If not enough drippings to make 4 cups, add chicken stock until liquid measures the amount needed. Bring drippings to a gentle boil. In a small bowl, add water to flour slowly; stirring until mixture is lump free. Slowly add the flour mixture to the broth, stirring constantly with a whisk or slotted spoon. If oil from broth comes to the top, skim and remove if desired for less fat content. Continue to stir gravy until thickened and bubbly. Add salt and pepper to taste. This gravy stores nicely in refrigerator for leftovers. Makes 4 cups.

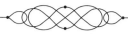
Time: 25 Minutes

ROASTED SALMON IN BUTTER/GARLIC SAUCE

Note: *This salmon is simply delicious, and even if you don't like salmon, you may just love this.*

¼ cup extra virgin olive oil

½ stick butter

2 cloves garlic, chopped fine

¼ cup fresh Italian flat-leaf parsley, chopped

¼ teaspoon crushed red pepper flakes

½ teaspoon coarse sea salt

¼ teaspoon coarse ground black pepper

1 salmon filet, 2 to 3 pounds

2 tablespoons fresh lemon juice

Peppermint sprigs

1. Preheat oven to 400 degrees. In a small skillet, place the olive oil and butter, and heat the two together until butter is melted. Place the garlic in pan and sauté on low heat only about 15 seconds, careful not to burn the garlic. Add the parsley, red pepper flakes, salt, and pepper and stir into the butter.

2. Spray a 13x9 baking pan with cooking spray and lay the salmon in the pan, skin-side down. Pierce the salmon with a fork in several places, and pour the butter/garlic sauce over the salmon. Bake for 12 to 15 minutes, or until the salmon turns pink and flaky. Remove from oven and with a flat spatula, lift salmon off the skin and onto a large platter. Drizzle the fresh lemon juice over the top and serve. Garnish with peppermint sprigs. Serves 6.

Time: 35 Minutes

ORANGE ROUGHY WITH VEGETABLES & ALFREDO SAUCE

Note: *Orange Roughy is a light mild fish that can be fixed simply, or like this dish with a wonderful Alfredo sauce. This fish will melt in your mouth.*

4 (4 to 6-ounce) orange roughy filets

Olive oil

Lawry's coarse garlic salt with parsley added

⅔ cup plain bread crumbs

½ stick sweet cream butter

1 tablespoon olive oil

3 cloves garlic, chopped fine

1 cup broccoli florets

1 cup thick-sliced mushrooms

½ cup thin-sliced carrots

1 teaspoon coarse sea salt

¼ teaspoon ground black pepper

1 tablespoon lemon juice

½ cup marinated artichoke hearts

1½ cups heavy whipping cream

¼ cup Parmesan cheese

¾ cup shredded provolone cheese

¼ teaspoon crushed red pepper flakes

1 tablespoon fresh curly parsley, chopped

Freshly ground black pepper

Curly parsley sprigs

1. Preheat oven to 400 degrees. Rinse fish gently under cool water; pat dry. Coat the fish on both sides with the olive oil and sprinkle with the garlic salt. Pour bread crumbs into a shallow plate and bread the filets lightly on both sides. Spray a 13x9 baking sheet with cooking spray. Place filets on baking sheet and bake 10 to 12 minutes, depending how thick the filets are. Fish is ready when it flakes with fork.

2. In large skillet, melt butter and olive oil and stir together. Add the garlic, broccoli, mushrooms, and carrots. Sauté vegetables until crisp tender, about 3 to 4 minutes. Salt and pepper vegetables while they are in the pan. Sprinkle vegetables with the lemon juice; add the artichoke hearts and stir in with vegetables.

3. Add the cream and bring to a gentle boil, then reduce heat. Stir in the Parmesan cheese and then the provolone cheese. Add the red pepper flakes and chopped parsley. Continue to stir until the vegetables and cheeses are creamy and smooth; remove from stove.

4. Remove orange roughy filets from oven. Place the filets on four individual plates and dip one-fourth of the vegetable cheese sauce over each fillet. Garnish each fillet with freshly ground black pepper and parsley sprigs. Serve immediately. Serves 4.

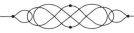

Time: 20 Minutes

PARMESAN CRUSTED COD

Note: *Cod is a delicate flaky white fish and is delicious almost any way you fix it.*
I think this Parmesan crusted cod is absolutely wonderful.

4 cod filets, about 5 to 6 inches long

Lawry's coarse garlic salt
  with parsley added

⅓ cup extra virgin olive oil

1 cup Panko bread crumbs

⅓ cup grated Parmesan cheese

2 tablespoons fresh curly parsley

2 cloves garlic, chopped fine

¼ teaspoon crushed red pepper flakes

½ teaspoon coarse sea salt

¼ teaspoon ground black pepper

3 tablespoons extra virgin olive oil

Freshly squeezed lemon juice

Lemon slices

Peppermint sprigs

1. Preheat oven to 400 degrees. Rinse cod filets in cool water; pat dry. Lightly sprinkle the cod filets with the garlic salt. Pour olive oil in a shallow pie plate and coat both side of cod filets in the olive oil; set aside. Make the breading by combining the bread crumbs, cheese, parsley, garlic, red pepper flakes, salt, and pepper.

2. Add the olive oil to the bread crumbs and mix together with your hands to form a moistened crumb mixture. Spray a 13x9-inch baking pan with cooking spray. Place the cod filets in the pan and place 2 to 3 tablespoons breading over the top of each filet, pressing the breading into the fish. Bake the filets uncovered for 10 to 12 minutes. The cod should turn white and flake easily.

3. Transfer the filets very carefully to a large platter and squeeze lemon juice over the top of each cod filet. Garnish the fish with lemon slices and peppermint sprigs. Serves 4.

SHRIMP SCAMPI WITH LEMON BUTTER

Note: *Shrimp scampi is an Italian favorite, and can be used as a main entrée or as a wonderful side dish.*

1 pound medium fresh or frozen shrimp, peeled and deveined

1 tablespoon olive oil

4 tablespoons sweet cream butter

2 cloves garlic, chopped fine

¼ cup fresh Italian flat-leaf parsley, chopped

¼ teaspoon crush red pepper flakes

2 teaspoon freshly squeezed lemon juice

Rinse shrimp in cool water; drain and set aside. Place olive oil and butter in a large skillet. Sauté the garlic for about 30 seconds, careful not to burn. Add the shrimp, parsley, and crushed red pepper flakes. Cook shrimp in sauce for 1 to 2 minutes, turning occasionally and being careful not to overcook. Shrimp will turn pink when done. Add the lemon juice and toss gently. Serve in shallow platter. Serves 4 to 6.

CAKES, COOKIES, &CREAMS

La Dolce Vita

La dolce vita means "living the sweet life" in Italian. Along with the good entrée, and our favorite pasta and vegetables, Italians always make room for the sweet things in life. It has been said that the sweet things make the bad things tolerable. This is so true after a hard day's work, when we humans just want to wind down with our favorite cup of coffee and a sweet. Maybe it is a biscotti, a cookie or two, or even a cannoli that takes the weight off our shoulders, even for a short time.

My father would insist on his sweet after every meal. If mom didn't have one made, he would toast her Italian bread and spread jelly over the top. But, more often than not, she always had something good in the oven. It was nothing for her to whip up a batch of Sesame Seed Cookies, or the Strawberry & Cream Cake made with her own yellow sponge cake.

She was a master with the Christmas cookies, and I have included my favorite story about this in the pages following. Do enjoy this section and consider the following suggestions:

1. Always have on hand plenty of baking pans; some of different sizes such as: 13x9x2-inch baking pans and 15x10x1-inch jelly-roll pan. Use store-bought aluminum 9-inch and 8-inch round cake pans. They do very well and the cakes will pop right out of the pans if oil sprayed and dusted with flour.

2. Plan on 9-inch or 10-inch springform pans for great cheesecakes, and 10-inch fluted pans for pound cakes. Don't forget the muffin pans and pie plates.

3. Purchase cannoli tubes either on line, or at your favorite kitchen store for making homemade cream-filled cannoli.

4. My favorite utensil is the Kitchen Aid electric mixer. This is a must if you want to seriously bake, and it will save you much time.

5. Watch for cookies, and be careful not to over bake them. Remember cookies still continue to bake after removal from oven.

6. Use lemon juice over fruit to keep fruit from turning brown.

7. Use real butter in all dessert recipes for the best taste and texture.

8. Cool cakes on wire baking racks right after removing from oven for 10 minutes, then pop them out of pans and let cool on wire racks before frosting.

9. Store soft cookies and crisp cookies in separate airtight containers. If stored together, the moisture from the soft cookies will soften the crisp cookies, making them lose their crunch.

10. Parchment paper is great for lining cookie sheets. The raw cookies can be placed right on the parchment paper, and the cookies will not stick.

Coconut Almond Cake
on page 211

Time: 1½ Hours

ROSALIE'S CANNOLI CAKE

Note: *This cake is not only beautiful but just as delicious as an Italian cream-filled cannoli. Topped with a whipped mascarpone frosting, the cake is just rich enough without competing for flavor.*

2 (9-inch round) layers, Pillsbury Moist Supreme yellow cake mix

1 (9-inch round) layer, Pillsbury Moist Supreme Devil's Food cake mix

Ricotta/Cream Filling

1 cup heavy whipping cream

½ cup powdered sugar

1½ teaspoons vanilla

1 (15-ounce) carton ricotta cheese

Whipped Mascarpone Frosting

2½ cups heavy whipping cream

1½ cups powdered sugar

1 teaspoon vanilla

1½ (8-ounce) cartons mascarpone cheese

Candied Pecans/Sliced Almonds

½ cup pecans, chopped coarse

4 teaspoons sugar, divided

½ cup sliced almonds, toasted

¼ cup raspberry preserves

Fresh raspberries

1. Butter and flour four 9-inch round cake pans. Prepare cake mixes as directed and pour batters into prepared pans. Bake as directed, careful not to overcook cakes. Remove from oven and place on cake racks for 10 minutes. Remove cakes and continue to cool on racks for about 1 hour. Prepare filling while cakes are cooling.

2. Make the ricotta cream filling by placing the whipping cream, sugar and vanilla in electric mixer. Beat mixture until thick and smooth, about 5 to 6 minutes. Fold in the ricotta cheese and continue to mix with a fork until completely smooth. Set filling in refrigerator for 15 minutes to set.

3. Make whipped mascarpone frosting by placing cream in electric mixer. Add the powdered sugar and vanilla. Beat on medium until stiff peaks form, about 6 to 8 minutes; add the mascarpone cheese and continue to mix on medium speed until smooth and thick. Place frosting in glass bowl and refrigerate until ready to frost cakes.

4. Place pecans in small fry pan with 2 teaspoons sugar over medium heat. Stir constantly until the sugar disappears and the pecans are candied, careful not to burn. Place pecans in small bowl to cool before garnishing cake. Toast sliced almonds in same fry pan with 2 teaspoons sugar; stirring constantly until lightly toasted. Remove and place in small bowl to cool. When both pecans and almonds are cooled, combine nuts.

5. **To Assemble Cake:** On large round platter, place one layer yellow cake. Place about 1 cup of the ricotta filling over cake. With large serrated knife, cut the chocolate layer in half. Place one of the halves over the filling. Add another 1 cup ricotta over the chocolate layer. Top the ricotta with the other half chocolate layer, and spread another 1 cup filling.

Top the second chocolate layer with the other yellow cake layer. Frost the sides and top of cake with the whipped mascarpone frosting, leaving a 3-inch circle on the top middle of the cake unfrosted for the raspberry preserves. With nuts in hand, press the nuts all around the sides of cake. Spread the raspberry preserves in the middle top of the cake, out about 2 inches. Apply dollops of frosting all around the outer edge of the top of the cake up to the raspberry preserves. Garnish with fresh raspberries and place a dollop of the frosting in the middle of the cake on raspberries in the center. Serves 16.

Time: 1½ Hours

BLACK BEAUTY CHOCOLATE CAKE WITH HAZELNUT FILLING & RICH CHOCOLATE FROSTING

Note: *This cake is a three-layer chocolate dream with a smooth hazelnut filling and a scrumptious chocolate satin frosting. Top it off with lots of chocolate curls, and every mouthful will lend a sigh of delight.*

Butter

Cocoa

1 cup sweet cream butter (2 sticks)

3 cups brown sugar, packed

4 large eggs

2 teaspoons pure vanilla extract

¾ cup cocoa powder

1 tablespoon baking soda

½ teaspoon salt

3 cups all-purpose flour, sifted and divided

1⅓ cups sour cream

1¼ cups hot water

Rich Chocolate Frosting

8 tablespoons sweet cream butter

1 (8-ounce) package cream cheese

8 (1-ounce) squares unsweetened chocolate, melted

½ cup cooled coffee

4 teaspoons pure vanilla extract

6 cups confectioners' sugar

3 (1-ounce) squares semisweet Ghirardelli chocolate

1 tablespoon butter-flavored Crisco

1 (13-ounce) jar Nutella Hazelnut Spread

1. Preheat oven to 350 degrees. Butter three 9-inch round cake pans; dust with sifted cocoa; set aside. In large mixing bowl, cream together butter and brown sugar on medium speed until combined and smooth, about 4 to 5 minutes. Add the eggs one at a time, beating after each one. Add the vanilla and continue to beat on medium for another 2 minutes until smooth and creamy.

2. Sift together cocoa powder, baking soda, and salt; add to the sugar/egg mixture and beat on low speed until combined.

3. Add 1 cup flour to the batter on low speed until combined, scrapping down bowl to make sure all the flour is mixed in. Next, add ⅓ of the sour cream, keeping mixer on medium speed and pausing to scrape down bowl. Alternate adding the flour and sour cream to the batter, mixing well after each addition and ending with the flour. While mixer is on low, slowly add the hot water until the batter is smooth and water is gone. Batter will be thin.

4. Divide the batter evenly among the three cake pans, shaking the pans to settle the batter. Bake 35 to 40 minutes, or until a toothpick inserted comes out clean. Remove from oven and let the cakes cool about 5 to 10 minutes. Remove cakes onto wire racks and let cool completely before frosting.

5. Make the rich chocolate frosting by creaming butter and cream cheese in bowl of electric mixer on low speed until combined, then on medium speed until creamy.

6. Melt chocolate squares in glass bowl in microwave until partially melted, about 10 to 20 seconds. Remove and continue to stir chocolate in warm bowl until completely melted and smooth. Add the melted chocolate, coffee, and vanilla to the butter/cheese mixture, and beat on low until combined. Add the powdered sugar, 1 cup at a time, mixing well after each addition until the frosting is smooth and satin. Frost sides and top of cake with generous amount of frosting.

7. Make Ghirardelli curls by placing chocolate and shortening in small saucepan. Melt chocolate over very low heat, stirring constantly until smooth. Next, pour the melted chocolate over the underside of a clean cookie sheet; spread the chocolate into a thin layer with spatula or butter knife. Place pan in freezer for 2 to 3 minutes, or until chocolate can still be lightly pressed with your finger tip.

8. Remove pan, and scrape the chocolate from bottom of pan with potato peeler or serrated knife. When the chocolate is just the right temperature, it will curl instead of break. If chocolate gets too soft, place back in freezer for another minute and continue until the amount of curls is desired. Lay curls on waxed paper and place back into freezer to harden. Spread curls over frosting on top layer of cake. Extra curls can be kept in zip-lock bag for another time.

To Assemble Cake: Place cake layers one at a time on cake pedestal or plate. Divide the hazelnut filling between the first two layers, extracting 2 tablespoons for top center layer. Spread the filling thick and even on the first cake layer, then place the second cake layer over the filling. Continue to spread the filling over the second layer. Using the rich chocolate frosting, frost the sides of the two layers before adding the third layer. Place the third layer over the filling of the second, and place the remainder two tablespoons of the Nutella filling just in the middle circle of the third layer. Continue to frost the remaining side and top edge of the third layer with the rich chocolate frosting. Spread prepared chocolate curls over the top of cake. Serves 12.

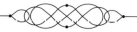
Time: 1 Hour

ROSALIE'S ITALIAN CREAM CAKE

Note: *This cake is not only scrumptious, but stands tall and elegant on your cake stand.*
It has been the rave among Italian desserts, and still remains popular.

Butter

Flour

1 cup buttermilk

1 teaspoon baking soda

½ cup butter

2 cups sugar

½ cup olive oil

5 egg yolks

2 cups all-purpose flour

1½ teaspoon vanilla

5 egg whites

1 cup shredded coconut

1 cup chopped pecan pieces

Cream Cheese Frosting

1 stick butter

2 (8-ounce) packages cream cheese, softened

4 cups powdered sugar

2 teaspoon vanilla

⅓ cup whole pecans

1 to 2 teaspoons sugar

3 maraschino cherries

½ cup shredded coconut

1. Preheat oven to 325 degress. Butter and flour three 9-inch round cake pans; set aside. Combine buttermilk and baking soda in a 2-cup measuring cup and allow room for the mixture to foam up; set aside. In mixing bowl, beat the butter and sugar until light and fluffy. Continue to beat on slow speed and add the olive oil slowly until blended and shiny. Add egg yolks one at a time and beat well after each addition. Add the buttermilk mixture and flour, alternately a little at a time, ending with flour. Stir in vanilla and blend well.

2. Clean beaters and beat egg whites until stiff. Fold egg whites into the batter with a sweeping motion, from bottom to top, and over again. Stir in the coconut and pecans. Pour batter into prepared pans and bake in oven for 30 to 32 minutes. Remove cakes and cool on racks for 5 minutes. Loosen cakes from pans and cool on racks.

3. Make the frosting by combining the butter and cream cheese in a large mixing bowl. Beat on medium speed until well combined. Add the powdered sugar and vanilla; beat until smooth and lump free. Make the candied pecans by placing pecans in small skillet with sugar. Stir over medium-low heat constantly, until the pecans take up the sugar and are toasted.

4. To assemble the cake, begin with the first layer, putting round side down on cake stand;

frost with the cream cheese icing. Continue with layers ending with round-side up. Frost the top and sides of cake liberally with icing. Place the cherries in center of the cake. Place the coconut around the cherries up to about 3 inches out and around the cherries. Place sugared pecans all around edge of cake. Makes 16 servings.

Time: 1 Hour

CHOCOLATE GANACHE
STRAWBERRY CAKE

Note: *This cake is a 4-layer chocolate delight, filled with strawberries and sweet cream.*
The batter makes 3 thick layers, so there will be an extra layer for you to frost and serve, or save for a later time.

Butter

Flour

1½ cups butter

3 cups sugar

4 eggs

5 (1-ounce) squares
   unsweetened chocolate

1 cup boiling water

2 teaspoons vanilla

3¾ cups all-purpose flour

2 teaspoons baking soda

1 cup buttermilk

Chocolate Ganache

2 (12-ounce) bags semi-sweet
   chocolate chips

2 cups heavy cream

Sweetened Strawberries

4 cups strawberries, sliced medium

⅓ cup sugar

Sweetened Whipped Cream

2 cups heavy whipping cream

4 tablespoons powdered sugar

½ teaspoon vanilla

1. Preheat oven to 350 degrees. Butter and lightly flour three 9-inch round cake pans. In large mixing bowl, cream butter and sugar with electric mixer. Add the eggs one at a time and beat after each addition.

2. In small saucepan, gently melt the chocolate over low heat, being carefully not to burn. When chocolate is melted, slowly add 1 cup boiling water and vanilla; stir until smooth. Remove pan from stove and let cool slightly. Add the chocolate to the sugar cream mixture and mix on low speed until combined and smooth.

3. Mix the flour and baking soda together and add the flour alternately with the buttermilk, beginning and ending with the flour. Pour the batter into the prepared pans and bake 35 to 40 minutes or until a toothpick inserted come out dry. Spray wire cooling racks with cooking spray to avoid cakes from sticking. Remove cakes from oven and let cool in pans for about 10 minutes, then turn out onto wire racks and completely cool before frosting.

4. Make the chocolate ganache by placing the chocolate chips into a heat-proof bowl. Pour the whipping cream into a small saucepan, and gently heat on low, being careful not to bring the cream to a boil. When cream has been heated through, pour the cream over the chocolate. Let the cream sit for about 15 seconds before stirring. Stir the mixture slowly until the chocolate is smooth and shiny. Makes 2 cups.

5. Wash and rinse strawberries; remove stems. Slice strawberries and place into bowl with sugar. Let the strawberries set for about 30 minutes to soften and become sweet. Drain off the liquid and use the strawberries to spread between cake layers.

6. Make the sweetened whipped cream by placing the cream in a chilled bowl. Begin mixing on medium speed, adding the sugar and vanilla a little at a time. Beat the cream until stiff peaks are formed. Makes 2 cups.

To Assemble Cake: Using a serrated knife, cut two layers in half to make 4 layers. Place first layer on cake plate and pour about ⅓ of the chocolate ganache over the layer. Spread the chocolate evenly over the layer, allowing a little to spill over the side. Next, spread about ⅓ of the strawberries over the chocolate. Next, spread some of the whipped cream over the strawberries. Continue to dress the layers in the same manor, ending with whipped cream and strawberries. Makes 12 Servings.

Time: 1 Hour

STRAWBERRIES & CREAM CAKE

Note: *Italians use a yellow sponge cake for this recipe, but I have found that a yellow box cake has a better taste. Filling the layers with strawberries and cream cheese gives the cake an elegant appearance.*

Butter

Flour

1 Duncan Hines Moist Deluxe Classic yellow cake mix

3 large eggs

1⅓ cups water

⅓ cup olive oil

1 (8-ounce) carton mascarpone
   or Philadelphia cream cheese

1 cup powdered sugar

1 cup heavy whipping cream

1 teaspoon vanilla

1 quart fresh strawberries

¼ cup sugar

Powdered sugar

1. Preheat oven to 350 degrees. Butter and flour two 9-inch round cake pans. In large mixing bowl, place the cake mix, eggs, water, and olive oil. Beat on medium speed until smooth. Pour batter into prepared pans, bake layers for 28-30 minutes, or until cake springs back when lightly touched. Remove layers when done and let rest for 5 minutes. Loosen the layers and place on rack until cool enough for dressing.

2. Beat the mascarpone and powdered sugar until creamy. Add the whipping cream and vanilla and continue to beat for 5 to 6 minutes, or until the filling is creamy and smooth; set aside.

3. Wash and drain strawberries; cut off stems and slice thin. Add the sugar and toss together; refrigerate for 15 minutes.

4. When layers are cool, place layers on counter top. With long serrated knife, cut the layers through the middle crosswise in half to make 4 layers. On large cake platter, place first layer cut-side down. Spoon a dollop of filling on the layer and spread evenly. Spread ¼ of the strawberries over the filling. Continue with the cream cheese/strawberry mixture for the next two layers, placing them cut side down. Place the last layer on top, cut side down, and garnish top with remaining cream cheese and strawberries. Sprinkle top with dusted powdered sugar. Refrigerate cake until set. Serves 16.

Time: 1 Hour

COCONUT ALMOND CAKE

Note: *This cake is a dream, very soft with an almond flavor and topped off with the traditional cream cheese frosting.*
See photo on page 201.

Butter

Flour

2 sticks sweet cream butter

2 cups sugar

½ cup olive oil

3 eggs

1½ teaspoon vanilla extract

1½ teaspoon almond extract

½ teaspoon coconut extract

2¾ cups all-purpose flour

1 teaspoon baking powder

½ teaspoon baking soda

½ teaspoon salt

1 cup buttermilk

1 cup shredded coconut

5 egg whites, beaten stiffly

Frosting

2 packages (8-ounce) cream cheese

1 stick sweet cream butter

5 cups powdered sugar

1 teaspoon vanilla

½ teaspoon almond extract

2 cups flaked coconut

⅓ cup sliced almonds

1 teaspoon sugar

1. Preheat oven to 350 degrees. Butter and flour three 9-inch cake pans; set aside. In mixing bowl, place butter and sugar, and beat on medium speed until combined and smooth. Add the olive oil and beat until fluffy. Add the eggs one at a time, beating in well after each addition. Beat in the vanilla, almond, and coconut extracts.

2. In separate bowl, sift together the flour, baking powder, soda, and salt. Add the flour mixture 1 cup at a time alternately with the buttermilk; beat until smooth after each addition. End with the flour, and fold in the coconut.

3. Using hand mixer, beat the egg whites until stiff. Fold the egg whites into the batter very gently from bottom to top until all incorporated. Divide batter into prepared cake pans, and bake in center of oven for 25 to 27 minutes. Remove cakes when lightly tapped on top and cakes spring back. Place on wire racks 10 minutes, then remove cake layers on same wire rack. Let cool completely before frosting.

4. Make frosting by placing cheese and butter in a medium mixing bowl. Beat on medium until fluffy. Add the powdered sugar 1 cup at a time, beating well after each addition. Add the vanilla and almond extract. Place first layer top-side down on cake pedestal. Frost layer and side with frosting, about ¾ cup. Repeat with second layer, top-side down. Place third layer top-side up and complete frosting cake. Take coconut in hand and press into the sides of the cake all around and on top.

5. In medium fry pan, place the almonds and sugar. Stir constantly over medium heat until the almonds become toasted and sugar disappears. Sprinkle the top of the cake with the almonds. Serves 16.

Rosalie Serving Best Loved Italian 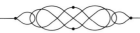 213

Time: 1 Hour

WHITE YOGURT PUDDING CAKE

Note: *This cake is like a mouth full of satin from the texture to the filling. The buttercream icing has the flavor of almond that gives it a wedding cake feel. Topped with shredded coconut, it is irresistible.*

Butter

Flour

5 egg whites

2 tablespoons sugar

1 box Duncan Hines Classic White cake mix

1 package (3.9-ounce) vanilla instant pudding mix

½ cup mild olive oil

½ cup water

1 cup Greek low-fat yogurt

1 teaspoon pure vanilla

1 teaspoon almond extract

Custard Pudding Filling

1 package (3.9-ounce) vanilla instant pudding mix

2 cups whole milk

1 tablespoon Greed low-fat yogurt

Buttercream Frosting

8 tablespoons sweet cream butter, room temperature

4 cups powdered sugar

3 to 4 tablespoons half and half

1 teaspoon pure vanilla

1 teaspoon almond extract

1 cup shredded coconut

1. Preheat oven to 350 degrees. Butter and flour two 9-inch cake pans; set aside. In an electric mixer, place egg whites and sugar. Beat on medium speed to combine, then on high speed until the whites are peaked and stiff. Remove egg whites and place in medium bowl; set aside.

2. Place the cake mix and pudding mix into the same mixing bowl; blend with an electric mixer on low speed to combine. Add the olive oil, water, yogurt, vanilla, and almond extract; beat on low to combine, then on medium until smooth. Stop the machine and scrape down the sides of the bowl with a rubber spatula. Beat for another minute; remove bowl. Fold the beaten egg whites into the cake batter with a sweeping motion, from bottom to top and over again, until the egg whites can no longer be seen. Divide the batter between the two prepared cake pans. Bake for 30 minutes, or until an inserted toothpick comes out clean. Remove cakes onto wire racks to cool. Prepare filling and frosting.

3. Make the pudding filling by placing pudding mix into a medium bowl; add milk and stir with whisk until smooth. Fold in the yogurt and place into refrigerator to thicken for 15 to 20 minutes.

4. Make the buttercream frosting by placing the butter and 2 cups of the powdered sugar in mixing bowl. On medium speed, cream the butter and sugar until smooth. Add the half and half, vanilla, almond extract, and the remaining powdered sugar. Mix on medium to high speed until smooth with a satin texture.

To Assemble Cake: Using a serrated knife, slice both cake layers through the middle in half to make 4 thin layers. Place the first layer on cake pedestal. Spread custard filling over the first layer. Place second layer over custard filling and continue to spread custard filling over layers. Place last layer on top. Frost the sides and top of cake with the buttercream frosting. Pat coconut onto the sides and top of cake. Place a cherry on the top. Makes 16 slices.

Time: 2 Hours

FRESH APPLE CAKE WITH CINNAMON WALNUT STREUSEL

Note: *This could be the very best fresh apple cake you have ever tasted. One bite will have you hooked, especially the crunch of walnuts bathed in cinnamon sugar. Yum!*

1 (10-inch) metal Bundt pan

Cooking spray

3 cups Granny Smith apples, peeled and sliced thin

½ cup water

1 tablespoon lemon juice

2 teaspoons cinnamon

3 cups all-purpose flour

1 teaspoon baking powder

1 teaspoon baking soda

½ teaspoon salt

2 cups sugar

4 eggs

½ cup mild olive oil

2 teaspoons vanilla

½ cup sour cream

½ cup dark raisins

Streusel Filling

⅔ cup sugar

5 teaspoons cinnamon

¾ cup walnuts, coarsely chopped and lightly toasted

Almond Glaze

1 cup powdered sugar

3 tablespoons milk

½ teaspoon almond extract

1. Preheat oven to 325 degrees. Spray Bundt pan with cooking spray; set aside. Place sliced apples in water with lemon juice to preserve color while preparing cake. In medium bowl, combine flour, baking powder, baking soda, and salt; set aside.

2. Next, place sugar, eggs, olive oil, and vanilla in mixing bowl of an electric mixer, and beat until yellow and frothy. Add the flour mixture to the egg mixture alternately with the sour cream; beat together until smooth. Remove mixing bowl to counter and fold in the raisins. Drain the apples and add cinnamon, coating the apples well. Fold the apples into the cake batter; set aside.

3. Make the streusel by placing the sugar, cinnamon, and walnuts in a small bowl. Sprinkle ⅓ of the streusel on bottom of Bundt pan. Pour a third of the batter over the streusel. Repeat with another ⅓ of the streusel over the middle batter, and continue with batter and streusel, ending with last of streusel over the top. Using a butter knife, swirl the streusel into the batter. Place pan in oven and bake for 1 hour and 15 minutes, or until toothpick comes out dry.

4. Remove cake and let stand about 10 minutes. Using a butter knife, loosen cake all around pan and also around the middle stem. Remove cake onto platter.

5. Make the almond glaze by combining the powdered sugar, milk and almond extract. Stir until smooth and when cake is cooled to slightly warm, drizzle the glaze over the top and rim of cake. Serve warm. Serves 16.

Time: 50 Minutes

OLD FASHIONED PINEAPPLE UPSIDE-DOWN CAKE

Note: *This cake is the ever popular pick for so many, especially the older generation who have fond memories of their mothers making this cake. Everyone loves this recipe!*

1 Pillsbury Moist Supreme yellow cake mix

1 cup water

⅓ cup mild olive oil

3 eggs

½ stick butter, melted

2 cups light brown sugar

1 (20-ounce) can pineapple slices or chunks, drained

8 to 10 maraschino cherries

¼ cup pecans, whole, optional

1. Preheat oven to 350 degrees. In large bowl, mix by hand the cake mix, water, oil, and eggs, just until all lumps are dissolved.

2. Coat the bottom of a 13x9 baking pan, or use 2 (9-inch) round pans with the melted butter. Add the brown sugar and spread evenly over the butter. Arrange the pineapple slices or chunks over the brown sugar. Place a maraschino cherry in the center of each pineapple ring. If using chunks, cut some of the big chunks in half and place the cherries in various places around the chunks. Place the pecans around the pineapple. Pour the cake batter over all. Bake for 35 minutes or until the middle of the cake springs back when touched.

3. Remove cake from oven and loosen sides with a butter knife. Place a large square platter over the cake and using both hands with pot holders, flip the cake over onto the platter. Be sure to hold the platter steady over the cake pan while flipping. Serve warm or at room temperature. Makes 12 slices.

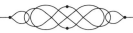

Time: 1 Hour

ST. LOUIS GOOEY BUTTER CAKE

Note: *The famous St. Louis Gooey Butter Cake was created in St. Louis, Missouri in the early 1940s. Two families claim authenticity, so we are not sure just who discovered it, but we do know it was, and still is, a smash hit. This cake is very gooey, rich, and exceptionally delicious! Although it is not of Italian origin, because it was born in St. Louis, it has been featured in many of the Italian bakeries located in St. Louis.*

1 box Pillsbury Moist Supreme Yellow Cake Mix

4 large eggs, divided

1 stick sweet cream butter, melted

1 teaspoon vanilla

1 (8-ounce) package cream cheese

4 cups powdered sugar

1 teaspoon vanilla

Powdered sugar

1. Preheat oven to 350 degrees. Spray a 9x13-inch pan with cooking spray; set aside. Place cake mix in mixing bowl and add 2 eggs, butter, and vanilla. Mix together on medium high; the batter should be smooth with a satin texture. Place batter in the prepared pan and spread to the edges.

2. Place cream cheese in mixing bowl; add half of the powdered sugar and mix on low to combine. Add remaining powdered sugar, the remaining 2 eggs, and vanilla; beat mixture on medium high until combined and smooth. Place cream cheese mixture over the cake batter. Bake in prepared oven for 35 minutes.

3. Remove cake and let cool 1 to 2 hours before cutting. Cake should be lightly golden and crusted on top and sides; be careful not to over-bake. Sprinkle powdered sugar over the top and serve with your favorite coffee. Makes 12-16 servings.

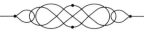

Time: 20 Minutes Prep
(Overnight Freeze)

ROCKY ROAD ICE CREAM CAKE

Note: *This cake is perfect for any summer gathering and feeds a large crowd.*

1 (10-inch) springform pan

3¼ cups chocolate cream-filled cookies,
    crushed and divided

⅓ cup butter, melted

1 (16-ounce) package semi-sweet
    chocolate chips

¾ cup evaporated milk

1½ quarts rocky road ice cream

1 quart vanilla ice cream

1 cup chopped pecans

1 tablespoon sugar

1. Place cartons of ice cream on counter to melt slightly. Place cookies a few at a time in blender and crush until cookie crumbs measure to 3¼ cups. Remove 2¼ cups of the crumbs and place in a large bowl, stir in melted butter. Place the buttered crumbs on bottom of springform pan and press crumbs over bottom and up the sides of pan, about 1 inch.

2. Make the chocolate sauce by placing chocolate chips in a small saucepan. Add the milk, and over low heat, melt the chips into the milk slowly. Stir constantly until the sauce thickens and appears dark and shiny. Place 1 cup of the chocolate sauce over the cookie crumbs and carefully spread over bottom. Place pan in freezer for 10 minutes.

3. Remove pan from freezer. Spoon out the rocky road ice cream in chunks and place over the frozen cookie crust; press down tightly with a spoon. The ice cream should be mostly solid.

4. Next, add the remaining 1 cup cookie crumbs over the rocky road ice cream and top with ¾ cup of the remaining chocolate sauce reserving ¼ cup for the top of cake.

5. Next, add as much of the vanilla ice cream as your springform pan will take. If you have a deep pan, you will be able to use the full quart of vanilla.

6. Lastly, toast pecans in a dry skillet with sugar for about 3 minutes over medium heat, stirring constantly. Remove from pan and spread the pecans over the vanilla ice cream layer. Drizzle the remaining ¼ cup chocolate sauce over the pecans. Place the ice cream cake in freezer for about 8 to 10 hours, or overnight. Remove cake from freezer and gently remove outer pan. Using a butter knife, loosen the bottom of the cake and place on large round platter. If planning to leave in freezer longer, cover top with clear wrap. Serves 16.

Time: 20 Minutes Prep
(Overnight Freeze)

SPUMONI ICE CREAM CAKE

Note: *Spumoni is a wonderful Italian ice cream, usually found around Christmas time. It is made up of three layers of chocolate, pistachio, and cherry-laced ice cream. This ice cream cake is not only beautiful, but scrumptious!*
I used strawberry ice cream for the color, however cherry ice cream can also be used.

1 (10-inch) springform pan

3¼ cups chocolate cookies, or chocolate biscotti, crushed and divided

⅓ cup sugar

⅓ cup butter, melted

1 (14-ounce) jar Hershey's chocolate sauce, divided

1 quart chocolate ice cream

1 quart strawberry ice cream

1 quart spumoni ice cream

1 (18-ounce) jar strawberry preserves, divided

Whipped cream

1. Place cartons of ice cream on counter to melt only slightly. Place cookies a few at a time in a blender and crush until cookie crumbs measure to 3¼ cups. Remove 2¼ cups crumbs and place in a bowl with the sugar and mix together. Add the melted butter and moisten the crumbs. (Set aside the remaining crumbs for later use.) Place the moistened crumbs on bottom of springform pan and press crumbs over bottom and up the sides of pan, about 1 inch. Place pan in freezer for 10 minutes.

2. Remove pan with frozen crust. Remove lid from jar of chocolate sauce and place jar in microwave. Microwave for about 15 seconds to bring sauce to a slightly thinner consistency. Pour ½ jar of chocolate sauce over the frozen cookie crumbs.

3. Beginning with the chocolate ice cream, place about ¾ of the carton over the chocolate sauce to form a layer of the chocolate ice cream. Next, sprinkle the remaining 1 cup chocolate cookie crumbs over the top. Next add the strawberry ice cream over the chocolate crumbs. The ice cream should mostly be frozen; tuck portions of the ice cream over the crumbs. The layers will not be evenly smooth, but will smooth out during the freezing process. Next, spread about 1 cup of the strawberry preserves over the strawberry layer of ice cream. If preserves are too thick, microwave for thinner consistency. Next, spread the spumoni ice cream over the strawberry preserves, as much as your pan will take. (The ice cream may go over the top of the pan slightly.)

4. Lastly, spread the remaining chocolate sauce around the rim of the pan over the spumoni, about 3 inches wide. Complete the inner circle of the center top with the strawberry preserves.

5. Place the cake in the freezer, covering the top with clear wrap. Let remain in freezer until solid, about 12 to 24 hours. Remove cake from freezer and gently remove outer pan. Using a butter knife, loosen the bottom of the cake and place on large round platter. Garnish the outer top rim of cake with pressurized whipped cream. Serves 16.

Time: 1 Hour

PUMPKIN CAKE ROLL
WITH CANDIED WALNUTS

Note: *This pumpkin cake roll is so delicious, it can only be explained by one bite.*

1 (15x10-inch) cookie sheet

Butter

Flour

3 eggs

1 cup sugar

⅔ cup solid packed pumpkin

¾ cup flour

1 teaspoon baking powder

2 teaspoons cinnamon

1 teaspoon pumpkin pie spice

½ teaspoon salt

1 cup walnuts, chopped coarsely
  and divided

1 tablespoon sugar

1 cup powdered sugar, divided

1 (8-ounce) package mascarpone cream
  cheese or Philadelphia cream cheese

½ stick butter

1½ cups powdered sugar

1 tablespoon lemon juice

1 tablespoon freshly grated lemon zest

½ teaspoon vanilla

Powdered sugar

1. Preheat oven to 350 degrees. Grease cookie sheet with melted butter and dust with flour. Beat eggs and sugar until thick and fluffy, about 1 minute. Beat in pumpkin; set aside.

2. In large bowl, sift together flour, baking powder, cinnamon, pumpkin pie spice, and salt. Fold the pumpkin mixture into the dry ingredients. Pour mixture onto cookie sheet, making sure batter is evenly spread. Bake cake for 15 minutes.

3. While cake is baking, place walnuts in a dry skillet with sugar. Over medium heat, stir constantly for about 2 to 3 minutes, or until walnuts are toasted and sugared. Remove to waxed paper.

4. Remove cake from oven and let cool for 10 minutes. Loosen cake around edges. Sprinkle a large clean kitchen towel with ¾ cup powdered sugar. Flip the cake onto the towel and gently remove pan. Starting from the 15-inch side, roll up cake and towel together; let set for about 1 hour.

5. Make cream cheese filling by mixing cream cheese and butter; add powdered sugar, lemon juice, lemon zest, and vanilla; beat until smooth.

6. Unroll towel and cake. Remove towel and place cake on cookie sheet. Spread ¾ of the cream cheese filling on the cake. Spread about ½ to ¾ cup candied walnuts over the cream cheese. Roll the cake up gently and place seam-side down. Spread the remainder of cheese filling across top of roll and sprinkle with remaining walnuts. Dust roll with powdered sugar. Makes 12 slices.

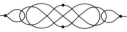

Time: 45 Minutes:

CHOCOLATE CREAM-FILLED CUPCAKES

Note: *These cupcakes are almost as heavenly as manna falling from heaven. From the rich chocolate frosting to the sweet cream filling, this is a rave review waiting to happen. Simply delicious!*

1 box plain Duncan Hines Moist Deluxe Devil's Food cake mix

1 package (3.9-ounce) chocolate instant pudding

4 large eggs

1 cup sour cream

½ cup water

½ cup mild olive oil

1½ cups semisweet chocolate chips

Sweet Cream Filling

1 (8-ounce) package mascarpone cheese

1 cup powdered sugar

1 cup heavy cream

1 teaspoon pure vanilla

Rich Chocolate Frosting

1 stick butter

⅔ cup unsweetened cocoa powder

3 cups powdered sugar

¼ teaspoon salt

⅓ cup whole milk

2 teaspoons vanilla

Sugar crystals

1. Preheat oven to 350 degrees. Place 24 cupcake holders in standard muffin cup pan. Combine both cake mix and pudding mix in a large mixing bowl; toss together. Add eggs, sour cream, water, and olive oil, and beat on medium speed until completely combined and smooth. Add the chocolate chips and mix in well. Place batter in cupcake holders and bake in oven for 18 to 20 minutes, or until top of cupcake feels firm to touch. Remove when done and set aside to cool.

2. Make the sweet cream filling by placing mascarpone and powdered sugar in mixing bowl and cream together with electric mixer until smooth. Add the heavy cream a little at a time until all blended; add vanilla. Mix on high for 2 to 3 minutes to a smooth consistency. Using a teaspoon, remove a deep cap from the top of each cupcake. Fill center with a tablespoon of filling. Return cap and frost.

3. Make the rich chocolate frosting by placing butter and cocoa powder in large mixing bowl; cream together until combined and smooth. Add the powdered sugar, salt, milk, and vanilla. Beat on low speed until mixed together well, then on medium speed until light and fluffy. Frost cupcakes and sprinkle with sugar crystals. Makes 24 cupcakes.

NOTE: If more frosting is needed, double the recipe.

Time: 1 Hour

PUMPKIN GINGER CUPCAKES WITH BUTTERCREAM FROSTING

Note: *These cupcakes are reminders of the fall season, and are rich with cinnamon, ginger and pumpkin. They are so delicious; everyone will want more than one.*

2 cups all-purpose flour

1 (3.4-ounce) package Jell-O instant Butterscotch pudding

2 teaspoons baking soda

¼ teaspoon salt

1 tablespoon ground cinnamon

½ teaspoon ground ginger

½ teaspoon ground cloves

2 tablespoons finely chopped crystallized ginger

1 cup butter

1 cup white sugar

1 cup packed brown sugar

4 eggs

1 teaspoon pure vanilla extract

1 (15-ounce) can pumpkin puree

½ cup dried dates

½ cup pecans, chopped coarse

Buttercream Frosting

1 cup butter

6 cups powdered sugar

½ cup whole milk or half-and-half

1 tablespoon vanilla

1. Preheat oven to 350 degrees. Line 24 muffin cups with muffin liners; set aside. In large bowl, place flour, pudding mix, baking soda, salt, cinnamon, ginger, cloves, and crystallized ginger; whisk together and set aside.

2. In mixing bowl, beat the butter, white sugar and brown sugar until light and fluffy. Add the eggs one at a time, mixing well after each addition. Beat in the vanilla and pumpkin. Next, add the dry ingredients and beat slowly just until blended. Remove bowl from mixer and stir in the dates and pecans. Pour batter in the prepared muffin liners to ¾ full. Bake in oven for 20 minutes, or until tops are golden and spring back when lightly pressed. Cool in pans for 10 minutes.

3. Make the buttercream frosting by placing butter and powdered sugar in mixing bowl. Set on slow speed to combine butter and sugar. Gradually add the milk until smooth. Add the vanilla and mix again until light and fluffy. Frost each muffin with buttercream frosting. Makes 24 cupcakes.

My Mother's & Christmas Cookies

When I was a child, I didn't recall my mother running around like a crazy person trying to cram in all the hustle and bustle of Christmas. There was very little shopping, not much decorating, and never over-exaggerated house cleaning. But I do remember the Christmas cookies. She must have started them sometime around October, because every time we saw her, she had her recipes out and a big pile of dough on the kitchen table. She would keep great big tin cans in her closet filled with all the treasured cookies of her homeland.

Every recipe was homemade, including all the famous Italian classics: Sesame, Italian Fig, Sicilian Slice, and Anise Cookies. She would also make her Biscotti, Pignolata (Honey Clusters), along with Italian Wedding Cakes, Chocolate Cherry Cookies, Italian Spice with Lemon Icing, and so many more I can't recall.

My father was a butcher and at my mother's request, he would bring home Styrofoam meat trays. Mom would fill these little trays with about 25 cookies, then wrap each one in clear wrap and like magic, these were her Christmas appreciation gifts to all her friends. She continued with this tradition with the list expanding each year. People in the community that served my mother, like church officials, doctors, office clerks, cleaners, hair dressers, neighbors and friends, all awaited "Miss Ann's" Christmas cookies. Without exaggerating, she probably made 10,000 cookies every year.

When she died in 1982, it was in the month of September. My older sister, brother, and their families, along with my children, knew we lost more than a mom and grandmother; we lost an Italian matriarch. Who would make the homemade ravioli and the homemade bread, or the pastas we all loved? But, above all, who would make the Christmas cookies? To say we were lost was an understatement, life could never be the same.

It was December 2nd, just three months after losing my mom, and I was in town getting some items for the holidays. I happened to run into her favorite butcher and when he saw me, he said, "So sorry to hear about your mom; we sure will miss her, and especially those wonderful Christmas cookies." I thanked him for his concern and wished also that she could be here, not only for him, but for all of us.

I was in the car driving home when I thought, "she is here, she is in me and in my sister and in my brother. Everything she lived for and loved was in each of us." I turned the car around and went back to the grocery store. Finding the butcher behind the meat counter, I said, "Can you sell me about 100 Styrofoam trays?" He looked at me and said, "How about I donate them to you?" Somehow he read my mind and I detected a teary-eyed gentleman.

Arriving home, I thought, "How can I possibly do this?" But determination is adrenalin waiting to be released. I quickly went to my mother's home, greeted my depressed dad, and said, "I'm taking mom's cookie recipes home." "Okay, honey," he said. The next three weeks became a bakery in my kitchen. I actually baked cookies every single day turning out batch after batch of Italian cookies. My dad spent every evening with me and was so excited that the tradition would be carried on.

With only five days until Christmas, the cookies were finally completed and the little trays were assembled and wrapped. I piled them in the car and brought them to all of our favorite community people. They had tears in their eyes as I said, "Your Christmas cookies, from Miss Ann's daughter!"

Not only did I learn to make the Italian Christmas cookies, but I became the matriarch for my family. I learned to make the ravioli, homemade bread, and the pasta they all loved. That Christmas in 1982 was a joyous one, one we will never forget. I know without a doubt that is was my mother's hand that guided me. I hope that you enjoy her recipes, and by all means, hold the traditions of your own family dear to your heart.

Rosalie

Excerpts from Rosalie's monthly newsletter that you can sign up to receive at www.rosalieserving.com

Time: 1 Hour and 15 Minutes

ITALIAN FIG COOKIES WITH BUTTERCREAM FROSTING

Note: *My mother, Ann Fiorino, would add these cookies to her Christmas cookie collection and hand out to friends for gifts. This recipe is very old and is a revered recipe to Italians.*

1½ cups dried figs

¾ cup light raisins

¼ cup silvered almonds

¼ cup granulated sugar

¼ cup hot water

¼ teaspoon ground cinnamon

Dash of pepper

2½ cups all-purpose flour

⅓ cup granulated sugar

¼ teaspoon baking powder

½ cup shortening

2 tablespoon butter

½ cup milk

1 egg

Buttercream Frosting

½ stick butter, room temperature

4 cups powdered sugar

2 tablespoons milk

1 teaspoon almond extract

Colored sprinkles

1. Preheat oven to 350 degrees. Put figs, raisins and almonds through food processor.

2. In mixing bowl, combine the sugar, water, cinnamon, and pepper. Stir into fruit mixture and set aside to be used for filling.

3. Combine flour, sugar, and baking powder. Cut the shortening and butter into the dry flour mixture until it resembles small peas. Beat the milk and egg together and stir into the dry mixture until moistened. Bring the dough together into a ball. On lightly floured surface, roll dough into an 18x16 rectangle. Cut rectangle into four 18x4-inch strips. Spread about ⅓ cup fig mixture onto the middle of each strip. Working with moistened hands. Spread the filling from top of dough strip to bottom, using a little more if needed. Roll the strip of dough over the filling to make a log. Tuck the dough under and seal. Cut each log into six 2½-inch lengths.

4. Place cookies seam-side down on ungreased cookie sheets. Curve each cookie slightly into a crescent shape. Snip outer edge of curve three times with kitchen scissors. Bake 20 to 25 minutes. Cool on rack and frost with **Buttercream Frosting**. Makes 2½ dozen cookies.

5. Make the buttercream frosting by creaming butter and powdered sugar, beating until light and fluffy. Add milk and beat until spreading consistency; stir in almond extract and frost cookies. Sprinkle with colored sprinkles while the frosting is still wet. Makes 3 cups frosting.

Note: This recipe can be made with fig preserves.

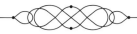
Time: 15 Minutes

ITALIAN PIZZELLE COOKIES

Note: *These cookies are Italian classics. They are also known as Italian wafer cookies and they are baked on a Pizzelle iron, which can be purchased at most Italian groceries. Pizzelles are eaten flat or folded into cones and filled with cannoli filling, ice cream, or any number of other sweets.*

3 eggs

¾ cup sugar

½ cup butter, melted

1 tablespoon vanilla

1¾ cup all-purpose flour

2 teaspoons baking powder

Olive oil

Powdered sugar

1. In large bowl, beat eggs and sugar until thick. Stir in the melted butter and vanilla. Sift together the flour and baking powder, and blend into the batter until smooth.

2. Heat the pizzelle iron, and brush with oil. Drop about 1 tablespoon of batter onto each circle on the iron. You may need to experiment with the amount of batter and baking time depending on the iron. Bake for 30 to 45 seconds, or until steam is no longer coming out of the iron. Carefully remove cookies from the iron. Cool completely before storing in an airtight container. Sprinkle the pizzelles with powdered sugar. Makes 24 cookies.

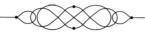
SESAME SEED COOKIES

Note: *Sesame seed cookies are an Italian classic favorite. They are not overly sweet, and have a tendency to get hard. They are perfect for dunking into your favorite coffee.*

3 cups flour

¼ teaspoon salt

2½ teaspoons baking powder

½ cup butter

1 cup sugar

3 eggs

1 teaspoon vanilla

2 cups sesame seeds

1 cup milk

1. Preheat oven to 350 degrees. In medium bowl, combine the flour, salt, and baking powder; mix together well.

2. Cream the butter and sugar with electric mixer until combined and smooth. Add the eggs and vanilla and beat until fluffy. Add the flour mixture a little at a time and stir into the egg mixture. Using all the flour and egg mixture, bring the dough together into a ball. Knead the dough on floured surface, adding a little more flour if dough is sticky. Pinch off small portions of dough and roll into a rope 8 inches long. Cut the rope into 2-inch pieces.

3. Put sesame seeds into a deep flat pie plate. Dip each piece of dough into the milk and then roll into sesame seeds. These should look like little logs, 2-inch by ¼-inch. Place on a non-stick cookie sheet, or on parchment paper and bake for 12 minutes. These cookies will continue to cook even after removing them from the oven. Makes 6 dozen.

Time: 1 Hour

ROSALIE'S SICILIAN SLICE COOKIES

Note: *These cookies were a part of my mother, Ann Fiorino's, cookie collection. It has been in my family since I was a child and I can still see them coming out of the oven, and eating them warm sprinkled with powdered sugar.*

1 cup Crisco Butter-Flavored
   shortening

1 cup granulated sugar

6 eggs

1 tablespoon vanilla

4 cups flour

4 teaspoons baking powder

½ cup pecans, coarsely chopped

½ cup maraschino cherries, coarsely
   chopped and well drained

1 (12-ounce) package semi-sweet
   chocolate chips

Confectioner's sugar

1. Preheat oven to 375 degrees. Place shortening and sugar in mixer and beat together until smooth, scraping down the sides of the bowl once or twice. Add the eggs and vanilla, and continue to beat until well mixed and fluffy.

2. Measure the flour and baking powder in a large bowl; sift the flour three times on wax paper. Place the flour back into the bowl, and make a well in the flour. Add the egg mixture and stir the flour into the egg mixture until partially blended. Add the pecans, cherries, and the chocolate chips.

3. With clean hands, mix the batter with the pecans, cherries, and chips until it comes together. Sprinkle flour on hands if the dough is too sticky and form the dough into 4 logs about 2x5-inches. Place the logs on a 12x15-inch cookie sheet lined with parchment paper, and place the logs about 2-inches apart to allow for spreading.

4. Bake the cookies about 22 to 25 minutes until golden brown. Remove logs from oven and let cool about 15 minutes. Slice the cookies and dust the slices with powdered sugar. Serve the cookies warm and soft, or let them harden for a tasty biscotti. These cookies freeze well. Makes 4 dozen.

Time: 40 Minutes

SUGARED PECAN BALLS

Note: *These cookies are so delicious, they will disappear before you can even serve them.
My kids devour them every Christmas and so will yours. Simply delicious!*

1 cup butter, room temperature

5 tablespoons granulated sugar

½ teaspoon salt

2 cups ground pecans

2 cups all-purpose flour

3 teaspoons vanilla

2 cups powdered sugar

1. Preheat oven to 325 degrees. Cream butter, sugar, and salt until smooth. Add the pecans, flour, and vanilla using your hands to mix thoroughly. Form dough into small balls and place on ungreased cookie sheet. Bake 15 to 20 minutes. Watch cookies closely; they are done when brown on bottom.

2. Roll the cookies while still warm in powdered sugar, being careful not to break. Place on cookie platter and sift additional powdered sugar over cookies. For a colorful Christmas cookie, add a few drops red or green food coloring to dough. Makes about 6 dozen cookies, depending on the size of the balls.

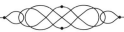

Time: 30 Minutes

ANISE COOKIES WITH ANISE FROSTING

Note: *Anise cookies are an old Italian favorite. They are soft little cakes the first day and begin to get harder the next day, perfect to dip in coffee. My mother always had these in her Christmas collection. This recipe comes from Ya Mamma's Restaurant, Merrimack, NH.*

½ stick butter, softened

¼ cup shortening

¾ cup sugar

2 eggs

3½ cups all-purpose flour

7 teaspoons baking powder

¼ teaspoon salt

1 tablespoon anise extract

⅔ cup light cream

1 tablespoon butter

2½ cups confectioner's sugar

¼ cup warm milk

1½ teaspoon anise extract

Colored Sugar sprinkles, optional

1. Preheat oven to 350 degrees. Combine butter and shortening in mixing bowl with sugar. Beat until smooth; add eggs and beat to combine.

2. In a separate bowl, combine flour, baking powder, and salt. Blend with a whisk. Add to butter mixture along with anise extract and cream. Beat until blended. Form into tea-spoon sized balls. Flatten slightly with palm, and place on baking sheet with parchment paper. Bake 15 minutes. Cool and apply frosting.

3. Make frosting by melting butter over low heat. Add powdered sugar, milk, and anise extract. Stir until smooth. Frost by dipping tops of cookies in warm frosting. Sprinkle with sugar sprinkles if desired. Makes 4 dozen cookies.

Time: 35 Minutes

CRUNCHY PECAN BISCOTTI

Note: *These biscotti are so delicious, your family will take them right off the cookie sheet as they pop out of the oven. I like them this way, and allow them to harden on their own, but if you want a true biscotti, then toast them on each side in the oven after they are sliced. I give credit to Southern Living 2005 Christmas Cookbook for this recipe.*

1¾ cups all-purpose flour

½ cup yellow cornmeal

1¼ teaspoons baking powder

¼ teaspoon salt

¾ cup sugar

1 cup pecans, coarsely chopped

1 tablespoon sugar

2 large eggs

½ cup olive oil

1 teaspoon almond extract

Powdered sugar

1. Preheat oven to 350 degrees. In large bowl, combine flour, cornmeal, baking powder, salt, and sugar; mix together well and set aside.

2. Place pecans and sugar in small skillet, and over medium heat, toast and candy the pecans. Stir constantly about 2 minutes until pecans are toasted and coated with sugar. Add the pecans to the flour mixture and stir in well.

3. Beat the eggs until frothy. Add the eggs, olive oil, and almond extract to the flour mixture. Mix together with fork and then with clean hands form the dough into three 6x2-inch logs. Bake on a large cookie sheet covered with parchment paper or on a lightly greased baking sheet. Bake for 22 minutes.

4. Remove from oven and let logs cool on the cookie sheet for 10 minutes. Cut the logs diagonally into ¾-inch slices with a serrated knife. If toasting the biscotti, return slices to the baking sheet and continue to bake for 5 minutes on each side, turning once. Remove and sprinkle with powdered sugar. Makes 24 biscotti.

Time: 15 Minutes

ALMOND ROSETTES

Note: *These little darlings will melt in your mouth, and are wonderful to serve any time of the year. They are especially nice for bridal showers. If you have trouble piping these, roll into small balls and thumbprint.*

1 cup sweet cream butter

1 cup sugar

1 egg

3 tablespoons half-and-half

1 teaspoon almond extract

½ teaspoon vanilla extract

2½ cups all-purpose flour

1 teaspoon baking powder

Sliced almonds

Powdered sugar

Preheat oven to 350 degrees. Place the butter and sugar in a mixing bowl, and beat on medium speed until mixture is combined and smooth. Add the egg, half-and-half, almond extract, and vanilla extract; beat until smooth. Add the flour and baking powder and mix in with the butter mixture until dough comes together. Transfer a portion of the dough into a pastry container fitted with a star or swirl tip. Lightly grease or use parchment paper on a large cookie sheet. Pipe the rosettes, about 2 inches in diameter, onto the parchment paper. Place a sliced almond in the center of each cookie. Continue to pipe rosettes until all the dough has been used. Bake 8 to 10 minutes, careful not to burn cookies. Transfer to a pretty tray and sprinkle with powdered sugar. Makes 3 to 4 dozen.

238

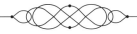

Time: 1 Hour

CHOCOLATE ALMOND BISCOTTI

Note: *These chocolate biscotti are wonderful with a cup of espresso or cappuccino and are great for dipping. The almond and chocolate are meant for each other.*

½ cup butter, softened

1¼ cups sugar

2 eggs

1 teaspoon almond extract

2¼ cups flour

¼ cup cocoa powder

1 teaspoon baking powder

¼ teaspoon salt

1 cup sliced almonds

1 cup semisweet chocolate chips

1 tablespoon heavy cream

1. Preheat oven to 350 degrees. Combine butter and sugar in a large bowl. Beat with electric mixer until light and fluffy. Add eggs and almond extract and continue beating until light and lemon colored.

2. In another bowl, sift together flour, cocoa, baking powder, and salt. Blend into butter mixture until smooth. Stir in almonds. Divide dough in half and shape into 2 logs, about 10x2-inches.

3. Place on lightly oiled baking sheet and bake for 30 to 35 minutes. Remove from oven and cool for about 15 minutes. Use a serrated knife and cut each log diagonally into ½-inch thick slices. Place slices back on baking sheet and bake about 3 minutes on each side.

4. Remove from oven and cool on wire rack. Melt chocolate chips and cream in microwave for about 1 minute, stirring until mixture is smooth. Drizzle the warm chocolate over each biscotti. Makes 36 biscotti.

Time: 1 Hour and 15 Minutes

HOMEMADE ITALIAN CANNOLI SHELLS

Note: *These shells are golden and crisp without preservatives and have a sweet taste. Fill them with ricotta filling and enjoy your own cannoli any time. Cannoli shell forms can be purchased at specialty kitchen stores.*

1¼ cups flour, divided

¼ teaspoon salt

1 tablespoon sugar

2 tablespoons sweet cream butter, softened

1 large egg, beaten

2 tablespoons milk

Metal cannoli tube forms, 5-inches long

1 egg white, beaten

4 cups olive oil

1 recipe **Cannoli Filling** on the facing page

1. Place 1 cup flour in a mound on a clean surface, large enough to roll dough. Add salt and sugar to flour and mix together. Work in the softened butter until the flour becomes mealy. Make a well in the middle of the flour and add the egg and milk. Work the flour into the egg mixture and bring the dough together, adding the remaining ¼ cup flour. The dough should be soft and pliable. Roll the dough out, turning often and sprinkling with flour to keep the dough from sticking. Roll the dough to a square about 12x12-inches. The dough should be very thin, about the thickness of a rolled noodle. Cut dough into 3x3-inch squares.

2. Place cannoli form diagonally on each dough square. Wrap pastry around form, one corner over the other. Seal corners with a little egg white.

3. In a heavy 6-quart pot, heat olive oil to 375 degrees. Deep-fry 3 shells at a time in the hot oil. Using a fork inserted into one end of the form, turn the shells once to brown evenly. These shells cook quickly in about 1½ minutes. Using the same fork tine, remove the cannoli from oil when they are golden brown and crisp.

4. Lay hot shells on paper towels to drain and let cool about 5 minutes. Gently hold forms with paper towel and push cooled shells off form (they will not break). Continue to wrap forms with dough and deep-fry until all the squares have been used. When completely cooled, fill each shell with cannoli filling. Dust with powdered sugar and serve. Makes 16 cannoli shells.

Time: 20 Minutes

CANNOLI FILLING

Note: *This cannoli filling is rich and sweet and can be used in your own homemade cannoli shells, or purchase ready-made shells in Italian stores. You will love serving this regal dessert!*

15 homemade or store-bought cannoli shells

1 cup heavy whipping cream

3 tablespoons sugar

1½ teaspoons vanilla

2 cups ricotta cheese

2 tablespoons maraschino cherries, drained and chopped fine

2 tablespoon small chocolate chips

1 cup chopped pecan pieces

Maraschino cherries

Powdered sugar

1. Place cream in large mixing bowl and whip on medium speed adding the sugar a little at a time. Add the vanilla and beat until stiff peaks form. Add the ricotta, cherries, and chocolate chips, and fold into the whipped cream.

2. Using a small spoon, fill cannoli shell first from one end and then the other. Press filling gently to make sure centers are full. Scrape ends to smooth filling and dip ends in chopped pecans. Garnish the ends with a maraschino cherry. Arrange filled cannoli shells on a large platter. Sift powdered sugar over the top of cannolis. Makes 15 filled shells.

Time: 20 Minutes

BEST OATMEAL RAISIN/ CRANBERRY COOKIES

Note: *While these cookies are not of Italian origin, they have so many things that Italians love, and since they are one of my favorites, I wanted to share them with you. Simply delicious!*

1 (15x10-inch) baking sheet

Parchment paper

½ butter

1 cup turbinado sugar

1 egg

2 teaspoons vanilla

1½ cups old fashioned oats

1 cup all-purpose flour

1 teaspoon baking powder

½ teaspoon baking soda

½ teaspoon salt

½ teaspoon cinnamon

¼ teaspoon allspice, optional

¾ cup raisins

¼ cup dried cranberries

1 tablespoon honey

1. Preheat oven to 350 degrees. Place butter and sugar into large mixing bowl. Cream together on medium speed until mixture resembles a thick sandy texture. Add the egg and vanilla, and continue to mix on medium until well combined. Add the oats, flour, baking powder, baking soda, salt, cinnamon, and allspice. Continue to mix on slow speed for about 30 seconds, or until mixed completely. Add the raisins, cranberries and honey. Mix again on slow speed for another 30 seconds.

2. Using a medium ice cream scooper, scoop the cookie dough out onto the parchment paper about 2 inches apart. Bake for about 11 to 12 minutes. Remove from oven and let cool on baking sheet for about 15 minutes. Makes 24 cookies.

Time: 35 Minutes

FRUIT PIZZA WITH SWEET CREAM FILLING

Note: *This fruit pizza is great to serve for parties, or just any time you want a real treat. The sweet cream filling tops it off.*

1½ cups all-purpose flour

½ teaspoon baking powder

½ teaspoon salt

½ cup butter-flavored Crisco

4 to 6 tablespoons milk

Sweet Cream Filling

1 (8-ounce) package cream cheese

1 cup powdered sugar

1 cup heavy whipping cream

1 teaspoon vanilla

1 cup fresh raspberries

1 cup blueberries

¾ cup strawberries, sliced thick

1 (15-ounce) can pineapple chunks, drained

¾ cup kiwi, sliced

Strawberry, left whole

Coarse sugar crystals, optional

1. Preheat oven to 400 degrees. Combine flour, baking powder and salt in a medium bowl. Cut in shortening with pastry blender or press between your fingers until mixture resembles coarse meal. Gradually add cold milk, stirring to make a soft dough that is smooth and workable.

2. Roll dough to ⅛-inch thickness on a lightly floured surface, about 13-inches around. Lift pastry into an 11-inch round tart pan. Press pastry into the already fluted edge of the tart pan. Prick bottom of pastry dough with a fork all over to prevent swelling. Bake 12 to 15 minutes, or until light golden brown. Remove from oven and let cool.

3. While tart is cooling, make the sweet cream filling by placing the cream cheese and powdered sugar in to the mixing bowl of an electric mixer. Mix on medium speed until smooth. Add the whipping cream a little at a time until all blended; add vanilla. Mix on high for 1 to 2 minutes to beat cream filling thick and smooth. Spread over tart crust.

4. Assemble fruit beginning with raspberries on outer edge of tart over the cream filling, placing the raspberries in a circle. Follow with blueberries, strawberries, pineapple, and kiwi. Garnish the middle of the fruit pizza with a large strawberry.

5. Sprinkle the fruit with sugar crystals if desired. Gently lift the tart from the pan and place on decorative round platter. Makes 16 slices.

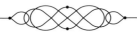
Time: 3 Hours and 15 Minutes

SFINGI (ITALIAN PUFF PASTRY)

Note: *This recipe comes from my sister-in-law, Rose Marie Fiorino, who has made these wonderful pastries for many years during Christmas holidays.*

2 cups flour

¼ teaspoon salt

1 teaspoon sugar

6 eggs

½ cup warm water

1 teaspoon yeast

3 cups olive oil

1 cup sugar or ½ cup honey

½ cup pecans, optional

1. Place the flour, salt, and sugar in a large bowl and make a well in the center of the flour. Beat the eggs until light and fluffy; set aside. Add the yeast to the warm water and let stand about 8 minutes, until the yeast begins to foam up. Pour the yeast water and the eggs in the well. Using a fork, mix the flour with the eggs and liquid until well blended. This dough will be very soupy.

2. Cover bowl with plastic wrap and let sit for 3 hours. The dough will rise to the top of the bowl and "bubble."

3. In a large deep saucepan, heat the oil. Drop a teaspoon of dough into the oil. If the dough puffs up, the oil is hot enough. Drop by teaspoons into the hot oil. The dough will puff up nicely and brown evenly. Turn the pastry once to brown the same on both sides, about 2 to 3 minutes total. Cook about 6 puffs or more at a time, depending on how large the saucepan. Remove with slotted spoon onto paper towel.

4. Sprinkle heavily with sugar while hot, or dip sides of puffs in honey, then in chopped pecans. These are best eaten warm. Makes about 4 dozen.

Alexandra with pie
ready for oven

CHERRY ALMOND PIE

Note: *This delicious pie is a favorite family recipe. I taught my granddaughter, Alexandra, to make it one Saturday afternoon and I snapped her picture right before it went into the oven.*

1 box Betty Crocker pie crust mix

2 (14-ounce) cans Oregon pitted red tart cherries

⅔ canned juice reserved

1 cup sugar

¼ teaspoon cinnamon

¼ cup cornstarch

⅓ cup cold water

2 teaspoons fresh lemon juice

½ teaspoon almond extract

¼ teaspoon red food coloring (optional)

2 tablespoons butter, cut up

Cinnamon Sugar

1 cup sugar

1 teaspoon cinnamon

1. Preheat oven to 375 degrees. Make pie crust according to package directions. Cut dough ball in half, using one-half of dough for the bottom crust and the other half for the lattice strips over filling. Roll bottom crust to fit a 9-inch pie plate allowing edges of crust to flow over pie plate. Do not trim. Prick bottom of crust with a fork and set aside.

2. Drain cherries, reserving two-thirds cup of juice in heavy saucepan; discard remaining juice. Add cherries, sugar, and cinnamon; mix together.

3. Dissolve cornstarch in water to make a thin paste. Add to cherry mixture along with lemon juice. Bring to boil over medium heat. Cook and stir until thickened and bubbly, and continue to cook and stir 1 minute. Remove from heat and stir in almond extract and food coloring.

4. Add filling to prepared pie crust and dot with butter.

5. Roll out remaining half of dough on lightly floured surface into a 12-inch circle. With pastry cutter, cut lattice strips about ¾-inch wide and 10-inches long. Lay strips in rows over filling, about half an inch apart. Use longer strips for the center of pie and shorter strips for the sides. Fold every other strip halfway back. Starting at the center, add strips at right angles, lifting every other strip as the cross strips are put down. Continue to add strips, lifting and weaving until lattice top is completed. Trim strips even with pastry edge. Fold bottom pastry up and over ends of strips and seal with a dab of water. Flute edges. Sprinkle lattice strips with 1 to 2 tablespoons cinnamon sugar.

6. Bake for 45 to 50 minutes, or until crust is golden and filling is bubbly. Serves 8.

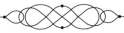

Time: 1 Hour and 45 Minutes

Sweet Potato Pie with Pecan Crumble & Marshmallow Meringue

Note: *I created this pie while working on my* **Rosalie Serving Holiday** *cookbook, and it was so good, I just had to include it for your pleasure.*

1 box Betty Crocker pie crust mix

1 (9-inch) pie plate

Filling

3 cups sweet potatoes, cooked, mashed, and lightly packed (3-4 large potatoes)

¼ cup butter, melted

½ cup white sugar

½ cup brown sugar

3 egg yolks

½ teaspoon salt

1 teaspoon cinnamon

¼ teaspoon nutmeg

1 teaspoon vanilla

1 cup half-and-half

1 teaspoon lemon juice

1 tablespoon grated orange zest

3 egg whites

Pecan Crumble

¾ cup flour

¾ cup brown sugar

1 teaspoon cinnamon

¾ cup chopped pecans

5 tablespoons butter

Marshmallow Meringue

3 egg whites

½ teaspoon cream of tartar

½ teaspoon vanilla

¼ cup sugar

1 (7-ounce) jar marshmallow cream

1. Preheat oven to 350 degrees. Place pie crust mix in medium bowl and stir in one third cup ice water. Stir pie crust mix and ice water until pastry forms a ball. Use entire packet for a nice large pie crust, cutting off about one-forth of the dough ball. Roll out crust and fit into a 9-inch pie plate with enough edging for a crimped border; cut off excess dough and discard. Prick bottom of pie crust with fork and set aside.

2. Boil or microwave sweet potatoes until very soft, about 3 to 4 large potatoes. Place into large mixing bowl. Add the butter, sugars, egg yolks, salt, cinnamon, nutmeg, and vanilla. Mix on low to combine, and then on medium speed for about 1 minute. Add the half-and-half, lemon juice, and orange zest; mix on medium speed until mixture is smooth. In another bowl, place the egg whites. Using a hand mixer, beat egg whites until stiff peaks form. Fold the egg whites into the sweet potato mixture until completely combined and smooth. Place the filling into the pie crust; set aside.

3. Make the pecan crumble by placing the flour into a medium bowl. Add the sugar, cinnamon, and pecans; stir together. Using a pastry blender, cut the butter into the flour mixture until the mixture begins to come together and crumble. Scatter the crumbles over the top of the sweet potato filling. Bake for 50 minutes or until a toothpick comes out dry. Place a large piece of foil over the pie at half-time of baking to prevent the crumbles from browning too much.

4. Make the meringue by placing the egg whites into a large mixing bowl. Add the cream of tartar and begin beating whites until frothy. Add the vanilla, and sprinkle the sugar a little at a time. Continue until whites become stiff; add one-third of the marshmallow cream and mix until smooth. Repeat with marshmallow cream, one-third at a time, until all has been mixed in with the egg whites. Place the meringue over the pecan crumbles and brown in 350 degree oven for 20 minutes, or until golden brown. Let pie cool and serve immediately or chill in refrigerator up to 24 hours. Makes 12 servings.

Time: 1 Hour

CHOCOLATE CREAM PIE WITH WHIPPED CREAM & CHOCOLATE CURLS

Note: *This could be the best chocolate cream pie you will ever experience. Paired with the real whipped cream topping, and shaved chocolate curls, your heart may skip a beat.*

1 box Betty Crocker pie crust mix

1 (9-inch) pie plate

¾ cup sugar

¼ cup plus 2 teaspoons cornstarch

¼ cup cocoa

3 egg yolks

3 cups whole milk

1½ teaspoons vanilla

2 tablespoons butter

Whipped Cream Topping

1 cup whipping cream

½ cup powdered sugar

1 teaspoon vanilla

1 small chocolate candy bar, room temperature

1. Preheat oven to 400 degrees. Prepare pie crust as directed and roll dough to fit a 9-inch pie pan. Prick bottom of crust with fork. Flute edges and bake for 8 to 10 minutes, or until golden in color; set aside.

2. Combine the sugar, cornstarch, and cocoa in a 3-quart heavy saucepan and stir together. Beat egg yolks and milk together and gradually stir into the sugar mixture. Cook over medium heat, stirring constantly with slotted spatula so mixture will not lump. Mixture will begin to thicken and bubble. Lower heat and boil one minute more, continuing to stir.

3. Remove from heat and stir in the vanilla and butter; stir until the butter is melted. Pour the filling into the prepared pie shell. Cover with clear wrap and let cool about 30 minutes, and then chill until firm.

4. Beat whipping cream until foamy, gradually adding powdered sugar and vanilla until smooth and sugar melts. Beat until stiff peaks form. Spread whipped cream over pie filling. Using a potato peeler, scrape candy bar curls over top and serve. Makes 8 Servings.

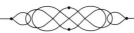
Time: 35 Minutes

LEMONADE PIE WITH SUGAR CRYSTALS

Note: *This pie is much like eating Italian lemon ice, but with a little more substance. It is very refreshing during the hot summer months.*

1¼ cups graham cracker crumbs

¼ cup brown sugar

⅓ cup butter, melted

2 (14-ounce) cans sweetened
    condensed milk

1 cup frozen lemonade concentrate

2 teaspoons grated lemon peel

½ cup heavy whipping cream

Pressurized whipped cream

White sugar crystals

Lemon wedges, sliced thin

Peppermint sprigs

1. Preheat oven to 325 degrees. Combine cracker crumbs, sugar and butter and press into a 9-inch pie plate. Bake for 8 minutes; remove and cool.

2. In large bowl, stir together the condensed milk, lemonade, and lemon peel. Slowly add the heavy cream and whisk together until smooth and creamy. Pour into crust, and bake pie uncovered at 325 degrees for 25 minutes. Remove and chill for 3 to 4 hours until firm.

3. Starting at edge of pie, flute canned whipped around a 3-inch rim. Sprinkle middle of pie with sugar crystals. Garnish pie with lemon slices and peppermint springs. Serves 8.

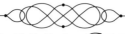

Time: 1 Hour and 20 Minutes

GHIRARDELLI CHOCOLATE CHEESECAKE

Note: *This chocolate cheesecake is everything you want in a chocolate delicacy. It is rich, creamy, and delicious!*

1 (9-inch) springform pan

1½ cups chocolate cookie crumbs

¼ cup sugar

1 teaspoons cocoa powder

¼ cup melted butter

3 (8-ounce) packages cream cheese

1¼ cups sugar

½ cup sour cream

3 eggs

1 (12-ounce) package Ghirardelli semi-sweet chocolate chips, melted

2 teaspoons vanilla

Chocolate Ganache

1 cup heavy whipping cream

1 (12-ounce) package Ghirardelli semi-sweet chocolate chips

Whipped Cream Topping

1 (8-ounce) carton heavy whipping cream

2 tablespoons powdered sugar

1 teaspoon vanilla

1 chocolate candy bar, room temperature

1. Preheat oven to 350 degrees. Combine cookie crumbs, sugar, cocoa powder, and melted butter in a small bowl; mix together. Place the crumb mixture into a 9-inch springform pan; evenly spread on the bottom and up the sides about 1 inch. Place the pan in freezer for 8 to 10 minutes to set.

2. Using an electric mixer, beat the cream cheese, sugar, and sour cream until smooth, about 3 minutes. Add the eggs one at a time, beating after each addition. Melt the chocolate chips over very low heat in small saucepan on stove; careful not to burn. Stir in the vanilla. Let the chocolate cool slightly and add to the cream cheese mixture. Mix on medium speed until the chocolate is well combined and smooth.

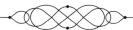

3. Pour the filling over the cookie crust and bake for 1 hour and 10 minutes, or until cheese-cake is set. Remove from oven and let cool for 1 hour. Run knife around side of pan to loosen cake; remove outer rim. Loosen bottom of pan with butter knife and place cheese-cake on platter. Prepare ganache and whipped topping.

4. Place heavy whipping cream in small saucepan and heat until very warm; do not bring to boil. Place chocolate chips into a small bowl and pour the hot cream over the chips. Let stand for about 2 minutes; stir until melted and smooth. Pour chocolate ganache over top of cheesecake and spread over the side.

5. Beat the whipping cream and powdered sugar until foamy; add the vanilla and continue to beat until stiff peaks form. Spread the whipped cream over the chocolate ganache. Make curls from candy bar with a sharp knife or potato peeler. Spread the chocolate curls over the whipped cream topping. Place in refrigerator for several hours until set. Serves 16.

Time: 1½ Hours

SHERATON'S FAMOUS CHEESECAKE
WITH PINEAPPLE SAUCE

Note: *This Cheesecake is a tradition with my family, and we make it every Christmas. Rumor has it that it was once on the menu at the exclusive Sheraton Hotel in St. Louis, Missouri, thus the name: Sheraton's Famous Cheesecake. Serve it plain or with your favorite topping.*

1 (9-inch) springform pan

2 cups graham cracker crumbs

¼ cup sugar

½ cup butter, melted

4 (8-ounce) packages cream cheese

4 eggs

1 cup plus 2 tablespoons sugar

1 teaspoon vanilla extract

1 (8-ounce) carton sour cream

¼ cup sugar

1 teaspoon lemon juice

Pineapple Sauce

1 (20-ounce) can pineapple chunks, not drained

2 tablespoons cornstarch

⅓ cup sugar

½ teaspoon vanilla extract

2 tablespoons butter

1. Preheat oven to 325-degress. Combine graham cracker crumbs, sugar, and butter in a small bowl; mix together. With the bottom of a cup or juice glass, pat the crumb mixture up the sides of springform pan, leaving a ½-inch crust on the bottom.

2. In large mixing bowl, beat cream cheese with electric mixer until smooth. Add eggs, one at a time, beating after each addition. Add sugar and vanilla, and continue beating until blended to a satin-like mixture. Pour filling over crust. Bake 1 hour and 10 minutes or until set in the middle. Cheesecake will form cracks on top. Remove from oven and let cool completely.

3. Loosen sides of cheesecake with butter knife all the way around cake. Remove outer pan from cake. With same butter knife, loosen the bottom pan from cheesecake and slide cake onto round platter. Make the sour cream topping by combining sour cream, sugar, and lemon juice. Spread evenly over top of cake. Chill at least 4 hours before serving.

4. Make the pineapple sauce by combining pineapple, cornstarch, sugar, and vanilla in a small saucepan. Stir to melt cornstarch and cook gently over medium heat until thickened. Add the butter and stir well. Remove sauce and let cool. Serve over top of cheesecake if desired. Makes 12 servings.

Time: 1 Hour

STREUSEL APPLE PIE WITH RAISINS & WALNUTS

Note: *This apple pie is so good and rich; you may want to have it with your favorite espresso.*
The streusel topping is crunchy and sweet with a little touch of dark raisins and walnuts mixed in with the apples . . . yum!
I have included my favorite pie crust which will actually melt in your mouth.

Melt-In-Your-Mouth Pie Crust

1¼ cups all-purpose flour

½ teaspoon salt

⅓ cup plus 1 tablespoon
  butter-flavored Crisco

4 tablespoons ice water

6 cups Granny Smith apples,
  peeled and sliced

¼ cup lemon juice

½ cup brown sugar

½ cup white sugar

⅓ cup all-purpose flour

1 teaspoon ground cinnamon

⅛ teaspoon ground nutmeg

⅓ cup dark raisins

⅓ cup walnuts, coarsely chopped

2 tablespoons butter,
  cut into small pieces

Streusel Recipe

1 cup flour

1 cup sugar

¼ teaspoon cinnamon

½ cup sweet cream butter

1. Preheat oven to 400 degrees. Place flour and salt in a bowl and mix together. Cut in Crisco until the dough resembles small peas. Sprinkle ice water over dough, 1 tablespoon at a time, and work in until dough begins to come together to form a ball. Flatten dough with your hands and roll dough out with a rolling pin on a floured surface. Using a flat spatula, lift, fold, and gently turn dough over to dust with flour and prevent sticking. Continue to roll dough to fit a 9-inch deep pie pan. Place in pie pan and crimp edges.

2. Core and peel apples. Slice thin and place in a bowl with the lemon juice; toss apples. In a smaller bowl, mix together the brown sugar, white sugar, flour, cinnamon, and nutmeg. Drain apples, and sprinkle the flour mixture over the apples. Add the raisins, walnuts, and butter and mix in with the apples. Spoon the apples into the prepared pie shell.

3. In medium bowl, make the streusel by combining the flour, sugar, and cinnamon; mix together. Using a pastry blender or with clean hands, press the butter into the flour mixture until it resembles small peas. Place the streusel over the apples and bake as directed. Bake uncovered for 45 minutes, using foil if needed half-way through baking if streusel browns too fast. Remove pie and let cool 15 minutes before slicing. Serves 8.

Time: 1 Hour

CRANBERRY/CHERRY TRIFLE

Note: *This beautiful dessert is mounded high in a trifle bowl with layers of white cake, white chocolate frosting and a delightful combination of fresh cranberries and cherry preserves. Top it with whipped cream, and show it off on your table.*

1 pedestal trifle bowl

1 Pillsbury Moist Supreme classic
  white cake mix

1 cup water

⅓ cup olive oil

4 egg whites

Cooking spray

Flour

Cranberry Filling

2 (12-ounce) bags fresh cranberries

½ cup water

2½ cups sugar

1 (18-ounce) jar cherry preserves

1 teaspoon almond extract

1 teaspoon cherry extract,
  or 2 tablespoons maraschino cherry juice

White Chocolate Frosting

6 ounces white chocolate bar,
  or squares, coarsely chopped

2 tablespoons heavy cream,
  or half-and-half

1 (8-ounce) package mascarpone cheese

½ cup sweet cream butter

1½ teaspoons vanilla extract

4 cups powdered sugar

White chocolate bar curls, or shavings

Whipped cream topping

1. Preheat oven to 350-degress. In large mixing bowl, combine cake mix, water, olive oil, and egg whites. Beat on medium speed just until blended. Spray and dust flour over a 9x13-inch baking pan. Bake cake for 26 to 28 minutes, or until toothpick inserted comes out dry. Remove from oven and set aside to cool.

2. Make cranberry filling by combining cranberries, water, and sugar in a heavy 6-quart pot. Cook cranberries over medium heat until bubbling. Continue cooking on low heat until cranberries pop, about 5 to 6 minutes. Remove from heat and stir in cherry preserves, almond extract and cherry extract, or the maraschino cherry juice. Set mixture aside to cool.

3. Make the white chocolate frosting by placing white chocolate bar and cream in small saucepan and melt over low heat, stirring constantly, about 4 minutes. Remove from heat and let cool. Place mascarpone cheese and butter in a large mixing bowl. Beat with an electric mixer on low speed until combined. Stop mixer and add the melted white chocolate, vanilla extract, and powdered sugar. Blend on low for about 30 seconds, then increase speed to medium until light and fluffy.

   To Assemble Trifle: Crumble cake into medium chunks and place a little more than one-third of the cake in bottom of trifle bowl. Next add one-third of the frosting over the cake. Add about 2 cups cranberry/cherry filling over the frosting. Repeat steps three times, ending with cranberry/cherry filling. (There will be cranberry/cherry filling left over.) The trifle bowl should be filled to the top. Garnish trifle with dollops of whipped cream all around edge of bowl; sprinkle shavings of white chocolate curls. Serve immediately, or refrigerate until later. Trifle will keep several days covered in refrigerator. Serves 15.

Time: 45 Minutes

TIRAMISU

Note: *Tiramisu is a popular Italian dessert and means "pick-me-up."*
You will love the mascarpone custard and chopped chocolate that laces this wonderful treat.

1½ cups strong cooled espresso coffee, divided

¼ cup sugar

40 Italian ladyfinger cookies

8 egg yolks

¾ cup sugar

1 cup heavy cream

¼ cup sugar

2 teaspoons brandy extract

2 (8-ounce) cartons mascarpone cheese

2 small chocolate candy bars, chopped or grated

Cocoa

1 cup heavy cream

¼ cup sugar

1 teaspoon brandy extract

Chocolate curls

1. Make the espresso coffee and add the sugar. Let the sugar dissolve in the coffee and let stand until cooled. Using a 12x8-inch baking dish, line the bottom with 20 lady-fingers on the first layer. Gently spoon half the coffee over the ladyfingers until soaked.

2. Beat the egg yolks in a large glass bowl for 8 to 10 minutes, adding the three-forths cup sugar a little at a time. The eggs will form a thick, smooth custard; set aside.

3. Using an electric mixer, beat the cream with the sugar until stiff peaks form. Add the brandy extract and the two cartons of mascarpone cheese. Continue to beat the cheese and whipped cream together until thick. With mixer on medium speed, fold the egg custard into the cream cheese mixture until well combined and thick. Pour one-half of the filling over the first soaked ladyfingers. Sprinkle one of the chopped candy bars over the top, and using a sifter, dust the chopped candy with unsweetened cocoa.

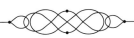

4. Dip the remaining 20 ladyfingers, one at a time into the remainder coffee. Very gently, to avoid breaking, place the soaked ladyfingers over the dusted cocoa. Repeat layering with the custard, chopped candy bar, and dusted cocoa over the second layer of ladyfingers.

5. This step is optional if you desire a top layer of whipped cream. Beat the remaining cream and sugar until stiff peaks form. Fold in the brandy extract. Spread over the tiramisu and garnish the top with the chocolate curls. Cover with plastic wrap and refrigerate 4 to 6 hours or overnight until all the flavors have settled and the cake is firm. The tiramisu can also be frozen and then cut for more solid servings. Serves 12.

Rosalie is also the author of *Rosalie Serving Country* cookbook. Available on ebooks, Amazon, and Barnes and Noble. Her first cookbook *Roaslie Serving Italian* can be found on ebooks.

Sign up for her monthly newsletter at *www.rosalieserving.com*

Rosalie is also a speaker, cooking class instructor, and hosts private cooking classes in your home.

Jeff and Tami

Nico, Regan, Alex and Bill

Capachino
and Rosalie

Bill and Rosalie